coffee
...made simple

This edition published in 2012
LOVE FOOD is an imprint of Parragon Books Ltd

Parragon
Queen Street House
4 Queen Street
Bath BA1 1HE, UK

www.parragon.com/lovefood

ISBN: 978-1-4454-9958-1

Printed in China

Produced by Ivy Contract
Cover and new internal photography by Clive Streeter
Cover and new home economy and food styling by Angela Drake

Notes for the Reader

This book uses standard kitchen measuring spoons and cups. All spoon and cup measurements are level unless otherwise indicated. Unless otherwise stated, milk is assumed to be whole, butter is assumed to be salted, eggs are large, individual vegetables are medium, and pepper is freshly ground black pepper. Unless otherwise stated, all root vegetables should be washed and peeled before using.

For the best results, use a meat thermometer when cooking meat and poultry—check the latest USDA government guidelines for current advice.

Garnishes and serving suggestions are all optional and not necessarily included in the recipe ingredients or method. The times given are only an approximate guide. Preparation times differ according to the techniques used by different people and the cooking times may also vary from those given. Optional ingredients, variations, or serving suggestions have not been included in the calculations.

Recipes using raw or very lightly cooked eggs should be avoided by infants, the elderly, pregnant women, and people with weakened immune systems. Pregnant and breast-feeding women are advised to avoid eating peanuts and peanut products. People with nut allergies should be aware that some of the prepared ingredients used in the recipes in this book may contain nuts. Always check the packaging before use.

In recipes that call for black coffee or strong black coffee, cafetiere or instant coffee should be used and made up with hot water to taste.

Picture Acknowledgments
The publisher would like to thank the following for permission to reproduce copyright material on the front cover:
Espresso © barbaradudzinska/Shutterstock images

coffee

introduction

Coffee is much more than just a drink to help jump-start your day. This much-loved stimulant is a universal favorite in cooking, and it tastes as good in simple recipes as it does in more complex, luxurious ones. Coffee has an intense, heady aroma and adds a nuttiness and rich, fabulous flavor to whatever you're cooking. Think of coffee as a versatile spice that can be used to season a whole range of delectable recipes, from dinnertime main courses to sweet treats for any time in the day.

This book celebrates the many creative ways that coffee can be used in the kitchen. Chapters cover small cakes and cookies, family cakes, desserts, savory (that is, unsweetened) recipes, and drinks. Here, you'll find an irresistible collection of tried-and-tested coffee recipes, from classic cakes to tasty sweet treats. Coffee can bring out the flavors of meats without imparting an overwhelming taste of coffee. It is also delicious in many drinks and cocktails, although you might want to use decaffeinated later in the evening!

These recipes use all types of coffee: brewed coffee, coffee and chicory essence (available online, or use coffee extract), powder and granules, and coffee-flavored liqueurs. For the best results and maximum indulgence, choose top-quality coffee to create a perfect dish every time. Refrigerate freshly ground coffee in an airtight container and use quickly because it begins to lose flavor after a couple of days. Keep whole roasted beans in an airtight container in a cool, dry place for up to two weeks, or for up to three months in a freezer. You can freeze leftover coffee in ice trays to use at a later date—in iced coffee or stews, for example.

When consumed in moderation, coffee has many health benefits and is full of antioxidants. It may also reduce the risk of developing type-2 diabetes, certain types of cancer, cirrhosis, and gallstones. So now that you know coffee can be a health food, too, there's no excuse not to find plenty of ideas in this book to use and enjoy it, whatever the time of day may be.

small cakes, bars & cookies

mini coffee & maple bundt cakes

ingredients

makes 4

1⅓ cups all-purpose flour,
   plus extra for dusting
1 stick butter, softened,
   plus extra for greasing
½ cup granulated sugar
2 eggs, beaten
2 teaspoons baking powder
1 tablespoon coffee extract or
   flavoring
¼ cup buttermilk

icing

1 cup confectioners' sugar
2 tablespoons maple syrup
1–2 teaspoons water

method

1 Preheat the oven to 350°F. Thoroughly grease four 1-cup bundt pans, then dust each with a little flour, tipping out any excess.

2 Put the butter and sugar into a bowl and beat together until pale and creamy. Gradually beat in the eggs.

3 Sift together the flour and baking powder in a separate bowl, then fold half the flour into the butter-and-sugar mixture. Fold in the coffee and chicory essence and buttermilk, followed by the remaining flour.

4 Divide the batter among the prepared pans. Place on a baking sheet and bake in the preheated oven for 25–30 minutes, or until risen and firm to the touch. Cool in the pans for 5 minutes, then invert onto a wire rack and let cool completely.

5 To make the icing, sift the sugar into a bowl and stir in the maple syrup and water and mix until smooth. Drizzle the icing over the cakes and let set.

coffee & almond cakes

ingredients

makes 6

1 stick butter, softened,
  plus extra for greasing
1 cup all-purpose flour
1¾ teaspoons baking powder
½ cup firmly packed light
  brown sugar
2 eggs, beaten
¼ cup almond meal
  (ground almonds)
2 teaspoons instant coffee
  granules, dissolved in
  2 tablespoons hot milk
2 tablespoons slivered almonds,
  toasted, to decorate

buttercream

6 tablespoons butter, softened
1⅓ cups confectioners' sugar
2 teaspoons coffee extract or
  flavoring

method

1 Preheat the oven to 350°F. Grease six ¾-cup mini loaf pans and line the bottoms with parchment paper.

2 Sift together the flour and baking powder into a bowl and add the sugar, butter, eggs, and almond meal. Beat with an electric mixer for 2–3 minutes, until smooth and creamy. Beat in the dissolved coffee.

3 Divide the batter among the prepared pans, smoothing the surfaces with a small spatula. Place the pans on a baking sheet and bake the cakes in the preheated oven for 20–25 minutes, or until risen, golden, and just firm to the touch. Let cool in the pans for 5 minutes, then carefully invert onto a wire rack and let cool completely.

4 To make the buttercream, put the butter into a bowl and gradually beat in the sugar, then beat in the coffee and chicory essence until smooth. Spread the buttercream over the cakes and sprinkle with the slivered almonds.

coffee & pecan streusel muffins

ingredients

makes 12

2 cups all-purpose flour
1 tablespoon baking powder
½ cup finely chopped pecans
½ cup granulated sugar
6 tablespoons butter,
    chilled and coarsely grated
1 extra-large egg, beaten
½ cup milk
¼ cup cold strong black coffee

streusel topping

⅓ cup all-purpose flour
2 tablespoons butter
¼ cup chopped pecans
1½ teaspoons instant coffee
    granules, finely ground
2 tablespoons raw sugar

method

1 Preheat the oven to 400°F. Line a 12-cup muffin pan with 12 muffin cups.

2 Sift together the flour and baking powder into a large bowl and stir in the nuts and sugar. Add the butter and stir with a fork to coat in the flour mixture.

3 Beat together the egg, milk, and coffee and stir into the dry ingredients. Mix lightly until just combined, being careful to avoid overbeating the mixture. Divide the batter among the muffin cups.

4 To make the topping, put the flour in a bowl and rub in the butter to make fine crumbs. Stir in the nuts, coffee, and sugar. Sprinkle the streusel topping evenly over the muffins.

5 Bake in the preheated oven for 20–25 minutes, or until risen, golden, and just firm to the touch. Cool for 5 minutes, then transfer to a wire rack and let cool completely.

irish coffee muffins

ingredients

makes 12

1 tablespoon sunflower or peanut
   oil, for brushing (if using)
2¼ cups all-purpose flour
1 tablespoon baking powder
pinch of salt
6 tablespoons butter
¼ cup raw sugar
1 extra-large egg, beaten
½ cup heavy cream
1 teaspoon almond extract
2 tablespoons strong coffee
2 tablespoons coffee-flavored
   liqueur
¼ cup Irish whiskey
whipped heavy cream,
   to serve (optional)

method

1 Preheat the oven to 400°F. Brush a 12-cup muffin pan with sunflower oil, or line it with 12 muffin cups. Sift the flour, baking powder, and salt into a large mixing bowl.

2 In a separate large bowl, cream together the butter and sugar, then stir in the beaten egg. Pour in the heavy cream, almond extract, coffee, coffee liqueur, and whiskey and stir together. Add the whiskey mixture to the flour mixture and then gently stir until just combined. Do not overstir the batter—it is fine for it to be a little lumpy.

3 Divide the muffin batter evenly among the 12 muffin cups (they should be about two-thirds full). Bake in the preheated oven for 20 minutes, or until risen and golden. Remove the muffins from the oven and serve warm, or place them on a wire rack to cool. If liked, slice off the tops and sandwich the muffins with whipped heavy cream, to serve.

after-dinner coffee liqueur muffins

ingredients

makes 12

oil or melted butter,
    for greasing (if using)
2 tablespoons instant
    coffee granules
2 tablespoons boiling water
2¼ cups all-purpose flour
1 tablespoon baking powder
pinch of salt
½ cup firmly packed light
    brown sugar
2 eggs
½ cup milk
6 tablespoons butter,
    melted and cooled
⅓ cup coffee liqueur
¼ cup raw sugar

method

1 Preheat the oven to 400°F. Grease a 12-cup muffin pan or line with 12 muffin cups. Put the coffee granules and boiling water in a cup and stir until dissolved. Let cool.

2 Meanwhile, sift together the flour, baking powder, and salt into a large bowl. Stir in the brown sugar.

3 Lightly beat the eggs in a large bowl, then beat in the milk, butter, dissolved coffee, and coffee liqueur. Make a well in the center of the dry ingredients and pour in the beaten liquid ingredients. Stir gently until just combined; do not overmix.

4 Spoon the batter into the muffin cups. Sprinkle the raw sugar over the tops of the muffins. Bake in the preheated oven for about 20 minutes, until well risen, golden brown, and firm to the touch.

5 Let the muffins cool in the pan for 5 minutes, then serve warm or transfer to a wire rack and let cool.

marbled coffee muffins

ingredients

makes 12

1/3 cup sunflower oil or
   6 tablespoons butter,
   melted and cooled,
   plus extra for greasing
2 1/4 cups all-purpose flour
1 tablespoon baking powder
pinch of salt
1/2 cup granulated sugar
2 eggs
1 cup milk
1 teaspoon vanilla extract
2 tablespoons espresso
   coffee powder

method

1 Preheat the oven to 400°F. Grease a 12-cup muffin pan. Sift together the flour, baking powder, and salt into a large bowl. Stir in the sugar.

2 Put the eggs in a bowl and beat lightly, then beat in the milk, oil, and vanilla extract. Make a well in the center of the dry ingredients and pour in the beaten liquid ingredients. Stir gently until just combined; do not overmix.

3 Divide the batter between two bowls. Sift the coffee powder into one bowl and mix together. Using teaspoons, spoon the batters into the muffin cups, alternating the coffee batter and the plain batter.

4 Bake in the preheated oven for 20 minutes, or until well risen, golden brown, and firm to the touch. Let cool in the pan for 5 minutes, then serve warm or transfer to a wire rack to cool completely.

coffee fudge cupcakes

ingredients

makes 28

1⅓ cups all-purpose flour
1 tablespoon baking powder
1½ sticks unsalted butter, softened
1 cup granulated sugar
3 eggs, beaten
1 teaspoon coffee extract or
    flavoring
2 tablespoons milk
chocolate-covered coffee beans,
    to decorate

frosting

4 tablespoons unsalted butter
½ cup firmly packed light
    brown sugar
2 tablespoons light cream or milk
½ teaspoon coffee extract or
    flavoring
3¼ cups confectioners' sugar, sifted

method

1 Preheat the oven to 375°F. Line three 12-cup muffin pans with 28 muffin cups.

2 Sift the flour and baking powder into a large bowl and add the butter, granulated sugar, eggs, and coffee extract. Beat well until the mixture is smooth, then beat in the milk.

3 Divide the batter among the muffin cups. Bake in the preheated oven for 15–20 minutes, or until risen, firm, and golden brown. Transfer the cupcakes to a wire rack to cool.

4 To make the frosting, place the butter, brown sugar, cream, and coffee extract in a saucepan over medium heat and stir until melted and smooth. Bring to a boil and boil, stirring, for 2 minutes. Remove from the heat and beat in the confectioners' sugar.

5 Stir the frosting until smooth and thick, then spoon into a pastry bag fitted with a large star tip. Pipe a swirl of frosting on top of each cupcake and top with a coffee bean.

feather-iced coffee cupcakes

ingredients

makes 16

1 tablespoon instant
coffee granules
1 tablespoon boiling water
1 stick butter, softened,
or soft margarine
½ cup firmly packed light
brown sugar
2 eggs
¾ cup all-purpose flour
1½ teaspoons baking powder
2 tablespoons sour cream

icing

1¾ cups confectioners' sugar
4 teaspoons warm water
1 teaspoon instant coffee granules
2 teaspoons boiling water

method

1 Preheat the oven to 375°F. Line two 12-cup muffin pans
with 16 muffin cups. Put the coffee granules in a small
bowl, add the boiling water, and stir until dissolved. Let
cool for 5 minutes.

2 Put the butter, sugar, and eggs in a large bowl. Sift in
the flour and baking powder and beat until smooth.
Add the dissolved coffee and sour cream and beat
until mixed. Spoon the batter into the muffin cups.

3 Bake in the preheated oven for 20 minutes, or until well
risen and golden. Cool on a wire rack.

4 To make the icing, sift ¾ cup of the confectioners'
sugar into a bowl and add enough warm water to
mix until thick enough to coat the back of a wooden
spoon. Dissolve the coffee in the boiling water. Sift the
remaining confectioners' sugar into a bowl and stir in
the dissolved coffee. Ice the cakes with the white icing,
then pipe the coffee icing in parallel lines on top. Draw
a toothpick across the piped lines in both directions to
create a feather pattern. Let set before serving.

mocha cherry cupcakes

ingredients

makes 12

3 ounces semisweet chocolate, broken into pieces

1¼ cups all-purpose flour

1¾ teaspoons baking powder

1 tablespoon unsweetened cocoa powder

1½ tablespoons instant coffee powder

2 eggs, lightly beaten

4 tablespoons butter, softened

3 tablespoons milk

½ cup firmly packed light brown sugar

24 fresh cherries, pitted

confectioners' sugar, for dusting

method

1 Preheat the oven to 350°F. Line a 12-cup muffin pan with muffin cups.

2 Put the chocolate in a heatproof bowl, set the bowl over a saucepan of gently simmering water, and heat until melted. Let cool for 5 minutes.

3 Sift the flour, baking powder, and cocoa powder into a bowl and add the coffee powder, eggs, butter, milk, and brown sugar. Beat with an electric mixer for 2–3 minutes, until smooth. Fold in the melted chocolate.

4 Spoon the batter into the muffin cups. Top each cupcake with two cherries. Bake in the preheated oven for 20–25 minutes, or until risen and firm to the touch. Transfer to a wire rack and let cool. Dust with confectioners' sugar before serving.

coffee crumb cakes

ingredients

makes 18

topping

²/₃ cup all-purpose flour
5 tablespoons butter,
    cut into pieces
½ teaspoon ground allspice
1½ teaspoons ground
    espresso coffee
⅓ cup granulated sugar
4 tablespoons butter, softened,
    plus extra for greasing
½ cup granulated sugar
1 egg
½ cup sour cream
1 cup all-purpose flour
1½ teaspoons baking powder

icing

²/₃ cup confectioners' sugar, sifted
1 tablespoon strong espresso
    coffee, cooled

method

1 Preheat the oven to 350°F. Grease a shallow 8-inch square cake pan and line with parchment paper.

2 To make the topping, put the all-purpose flour, butter, allspice, and coffee in a food processor or blender and process until the mixture starts to resemble coarse bread crumbs. Add the granulated sugar and process again briefly. Transfer the mixture to a mixing bowl.

3 To make the cake, put the butter, granulated sugar, egg, and sour cream in the food processor or blender. Sift in the flour and baking powder, then process until smooth and creamy. Transfer to the pan and smooth level with a spatula. Sprinkle the topping evenly over the top. Bake in the preheated oven for 30–35 minutes, or until risen and firm to the touch and a toothpick inserted into the center comes out clean. Let cool in the pan for 10 minutes, then transfer to a wire rack to cool completely.

4 To make the icing, put all but 2 tablespoons of the confectioners' sugar in a small mixing bowl and add the coffee. Beat to a smooth paste that falls in a thick trail from the spoon, adding a little more confectioners' sugar, if necessary. Cut the cake into three even pieces, then cut across to make 18 rectangular pieces. Drizzle with the icing.

mocha raspberry crumb bars

ingredients

makes 8

1½ sticks butter, softened,
    plus extra for greasing
2 cups all-purpose flour, sifted
1½ tablespoons instant
    coffee powder
½ cup granulated sugar
⅓ cup raspberry preserves
⅓ cup chopped mixed nuts
2 tablespoons raw sugar

method

1 Preheat the oven to 350°F. Grease a shallow 8-inch square cake pan and line with parchment paper.

2 Put the butter, flour, instant coffee powder, and granulated sugar into a food processor or blender and process for a few seconds until the mixture starts to clump together.

3 Press three-quarters of the shortbread dough into the bottom of the prepared pan in an even layer. Smooth level with a spatula.

4 Bake in the preheated oven for 20 minutes, or until pale golden. Remove from the oven and let cool for 5 minutes. Spread the preserves over the shortbread layer. Mix the nuts and raw sugar into the remaining shortbread dough and sprinkle it over the preserves, pressing down gently.

5 Return to the oven for an additional 20–25 minutes, or until the topping is golden brown. Let cool completely in the pan, then remove and cut into eight bars.

variation

Replace the raspberry preserves with apricot preserves or blueberry preserves.

cinnamon coffee rolls

ingredients

makes 9

3¼ cups white bread flour,
   plus extra for dusting
¼ teaspoon salt
1½ teaspoons active dry yeast
¼ cup granulated sugar
4 tablespoons butter, melted,
   plus extra for greasing
1 egg, beaten
1 cup lukewarm milk
oil, for greasing
1 cup confectioners' sugar,
   mixed to a smooth icing
   with 1 tablespoon water,
   to decorate

filling

3 tablespoons butter, softened
¼ cup firmly packed dark
   brown sugar
1½ teaspoons instant coffee
   granules, finely ground
1 teaspoon ground cinnamon

method

1 Sift the flour and salt into a large bowl. Stir in the yeast and sugar and make a well in the center. Beat together the butter, egg, and milk in another bowl, then pour into the well and mix to a dough. Turn out the dough onto a lightly floured surface and knead for 5–6 minutes, until smooth and elastic, adding more flour if it is too sticky. Place the dough in a bowl, cover with lightly oiled plastic wrap, and let rest in a warm place for 1½ hours, or until doubled in size. Grease a 9-inch square cake pan.

2 Turn out the dough onto a floured surface and lightly knead for 1 minute. Roll out to a 12-inch square. To make the filling, spread the butter over the dough. Mix together the sugar, coffee, and cinnamon and sprinkle over the butter in an even layer. Roll up the dough from one side. Using a sharp knife, cut into nine circles and place the rolls, cut-side up, in the prepared pan. Cover loosely with oiled plastic wrap and let rest for 40–50 minutes, or until doubled in size. Meanwhile, preheat the oven to 400°F.

3 Bake the rolls in the preheated oven for 18–20 minutes, or until risen and golden. Let cool for 10 minutes in the pan, then invert onto a wire rack to cool completely.

4 Drizzle the icing over the rolls, let set, then pull apart to serve.

coffee caramel éclairs

ingredients

makes 12

choux dough

⅔ cup water
4 tablespoons butter,
    plus extra for greasing
½ cup all-purpose flour, sifted
2 eggs, lightly beaten

filling

1¼ cups heavy cream
¼ cup rum
1 tablespoon confectioners' sugar

coffee caramel

1 cup granulated sugar
½ cup water
1 teaspoon instant coffee

method

1 Put the water and butter in a saucepan and heat gently until the butter melts, then turn up the heat and bring it rapidly to a boil. Immediately add all the flour, remove the pan from the heat, and stir the mixture into a paste that leaves the sides of the pan clean.

2 Meanwhile, preheat the oven to 425°F. Grease a baking sheet and prepare a pastry bag fitted with a plain ¾-inch tip. Gradually beat the eggs into the flour paste and continue beating until it is smooth and glossy. Spoon the paste into the bag and pipe 12 strips of paste on the baking sheet.

3 Bake for 15 minutes. Reduce the oven temperature to 375°F and cook for an additional 20–25 minutes, until the éclairs are risen, browned, and crisp. Transfer to a wire rack, slitting each pastry lengthwise along the side to let steam escape. Let cool.

4 Whip the cream with the rum and confectioners' sugar. Pipe into the pastries and place them close together on the wire rack, putting it over a baking sheet.

5 Put the sugar in a saucepan and add the water. Heat gently until the sugar has dissolved. Bring to a boil and boil rapidly, without stirring, until the syrup turns golden. Remove from the heat and stir in the coffee using a metal fork. Drizzle over the éclairs. Let set and cool.

cappuccino squares

ingredients

makes 15

2 sticks butter, softened,
   plus extra for greasing
1³⁄₄ cups all-purpose flour
3¹⁄₂ teaspoons baking powder
1 teaspoon unsweetened cocoa
   powder, plus extra for dusting
1 cup granulated sugar
4 eggs, beaten
3 tablespoons instant coffee
   powder, dissolved in
   2 tablespoons hot water

white chocolate frosting

4 ounces white chocolate,
   broken into pieces
4 tablespoons butter, softened
3 tablespoons milk
1¹⁄₃ cups confectioners' sugar

method

1 Preheat the oven to 350°F. Lightly grease and line the bottom of a shallow 11 x 7-inch cake pan.

2 Sift the flour, baking powder, and cocoa into a bowl and add the butter, granulated sugar, eggs, and coffee. Beat well, by hand or using an electric mixer, until smooth, then spoon the batter into the prepared pan and smooth the surface with a spatula.

3 Bake in the preheated oven for 35–40 minutes, or until risen and firm to the touch, then invert onto a wire rack and let cool completely.

4 To make the frosting, put the chocolate, butter, and milk in a heatproof bowl set over a saucepan of simmering water and stir until the chocolate has melted. Remove the bowl from the pan and sift in the confectioners' sugar. Beat until smooth, then spread over the cake. Dust the top of the cake with sifted cocoa, then cut into squares.

variation

To make a coffee frosting, substitute 2–3 teaspoons instant coffee for the white chocolate.

coffee madeleines

ingredients

makes 12

3 tablespoons butter, melted,
   plus extra for greasing
½ cup all-purpose flour,
   plus extra for dusting
1 extra-large egg
¼ cup granulated sugar
1 teaspoon coffee extract or
   flavoring
½ teaspoon baking powder

icing
⅔ cup confectioners' sugar, sifted
4–5 teaspoons strong black coffee

method

1 Preheat the oven to 375°F. Grease a 12-cup madeleine pan with butter, then lightly dust with flour, tipping out any excess.

2 Put the egg, sugar, and coffee into a heatproof bowl set over a saucepan of simmering water. Beat with an electric mixer until the mixture is thick and pale and leaves a trail on the surface when the beaters are lifted.

3 Sift the flour and baking powder. Add half the flour mixture to the egg-sugar mixture and fold in gently, then pour over half the butter and fold in until just incorporated. Repeat with the remaining flour mixture and butter.

4 Spoon the batter into the prepared pan, being careful to avoid overfilling the cups. Bake in the preheated oven for 8–10 minutes, or until risen and springy to the touch. Let cool in the pan for 5 minutes, then turn out onto a wire rack and let cool completely.

5 To make the icing, put the sugar and coffee in a small bowl and beat together until smooth. Dip each madeleine in the icing to coat just halfway. Let set on a wire rack.

marbled mocha whoopie pies

ingredients

makes 10

2 cups all-purpose flour
1 teaspoon baking soda
large pinch of salt
1 stick butter, softened
¾ cup granulated sugar
1 extra-large egg, beaten
⅔ cup buttermilk
1 teaspoon vanilla extract
1 teaspoon cold strong black coffee
  or coffee extract
1 tablespoon unsweetened
  cocoa powder

chocolate & cream filling

5 ounces semisweet chocolate,
  finely chopped
2 cups heavy cream
1 tablespoon strong black coffee,
  cooled

method

1 Preheat the oven to 350°F. Line two to three large baking sheets with parchment paper. Sift the all-purpose flour, baking soda, and salt.

2 Put the butter and sugar in a bowl and beat with an electric mixer until pale and fluffy. Beat in the egg, then half the flour mixture, and, finally, the buttermilk. Stir in the rest of the flour, reserving 1 tablespoon. Transfer half the batter to a second bowl. Stir the vanilla extract and remaining tablespoon of flour mixture into one bowl. Stir the coffee and cocoa powder into the second bowl. Swirl the two batters together to create a marbled effect.

3 Spoon 20 mounds of the batter onto the baking sheets, spaced well apart. Bake in the preheated oven, one sheet at a time, for 10–12 minutes, until risen and just firm to the touch. Let cool for 5 minutes, then transfer to a wire rack and let cool completely.

4 Put the chocolate in a heatproof bowl. Heat 1 cup of the cream and the coffee in a saucepan until boiling, then pour over the chocolate and stir until the chocolate has melted. Let cool for 20–30 minutes, stirring occasionally, until thickened. Whip the rest of the cream into firm peaks. Spread the chocolate mixture on the flat side of half of the cakes and top with the whipped cream. Top with the rest of the cakes.

coffee cream macaroons

ingredients

makes 16

¾ cup almond meal
    (ground almonds)
1 teaspoon coffee granules,
    finely crushed
1 cup confectioners' sugar
2 extra-large egg whites
¼ cup superfine sugar or
    granulated sugar
1 tablespoon amber sugar crystals,
    lightly crushed

filling

½ cup cream cheese
2 tablespoons unsalted
    butter, softened
2 teaspoons strong black
    coffee, cooled
1 cup confectioners' sugar, sifted

method

1 Line two baking sheets with parchment paper. Put the almond meal, coffee granules, and confectioners' sugar in a food processor or blender and process for 15 seconds. Sift the mixture into a bowl.

2 Put the egg whites in a large bowl and beat until they form soft peaks. Gradually beat in the superfine sugar to make a firm, glossy meringue. Using a spatula, fold the almond mixture into the meringue, one-third at a time. Continue to cut and fold the mixture until it forms a shiny batter with a thick, ribbon-like consistency.

3 Pour the mixture into a pastry bag fitted with a ½-inch plain tip. Pipe 32 small circles onto the prepared baking sheets. Tap the baking sheets firmly on a work surface to remove air bubbles. Sprinkle over the sugar crystals. Let stand at room temperature for 30 minutes. Preheat the oven to 325°F.

4 Bake in the preheated oven for 10–15 minutes. Cool for 10 minutes, then carefully peel the macaroons off the parchment paper. Let cool completely.

5 To make the filling, put all the ingredients in a bowl and, using an electric mixer, beat until smooth. Use to sandwich together pairs of macaroons.

coffee cream & walnut cookies

ingredients

makes about 30

2 sticks butter, softened
¾ cup granulated sugar
1 egg yolk, lightly beaten
2 teaspoons vanilla extract
1¾ cups all-purpose flour
pinch of salt
⅔ cup ground walnuts
½ cup finely chopped walnuts

coffee cream

6 tablespoons butter, softened
1¼ cups confectioners' sugar
1½ teaspoons strong black
    coffee, cooled

method

1 Put the butter and sugar in a large bowl and beat together until light and fluffy, then beat in the egg yolk and vanilla extract. Sift the flour and salt into the mixture, add the ground walnuts, and stir until combined. Halve the dough, shape into balls, wrap in plastic wrap, and chill in the refrigerator for 30–60 minutes.

2 Preheat the oven to 375°F. Line two baking sheets with parchment paper. Unwrap the dough and roll out between two sheets of parchment paper. Cut out cookies with a 2½-inch fluted circle cutter and place them on the baking sheets, spaced well apart.

3 Bake in the preheated oven for 10–15 minutes, or until light golden brown. Let cool on the baking sheets for 5–10 minutes, then transfer the cookies to wire racks to cool completely.

4 To make the coffee cream, beat the butter and confectioners' sugar in a bowl until smooth and thoroughly combined, then beat in the coffee. Sandwich together the cookies in pairs with the coffee cream, pressing gently so that the cream oozes out of the sides. Smooth the sides with a dampened finger. Spread out the chopped walnuts in a shallow dish and roll the cookies in them to coat the sides of the filling.

mocha walnut cookies

ingredients

makes about 16

1 stick butter, softened,
　　plus extra for greasing
½ cup firmly packed light
　　brown sugar
⅓ cup granulated sugar
1 teaspoon vanilla extract
1 tablespoon instant coffee
　　granules, dissolved in
　　1 tablespoon hot water
1 egg
1⅓ cups all-purpose flour
½ teaspoon baking powder
¼ teaspoon baking soda
⅓ cup milk chocolate chips
½ cup coarsely chopped walnuts

method

1 Preheat the oven to 350°F and grease two large baking sheets.

2 Put the butter and sugars in a large bowl and beat together until light and fluffy. Put the vanilla extract, coffee, and egg in a separate bowl and beat together. Gradually add the coffee mixture to the butter and sugar, beating until fluffy. Sift the flour, baking powder, and baking soda into the mixture and fold in carefully. Fold in the chocolate chips and walnuts.

3 Spoon heaping teaspoons of the dough onto the prepared baking sheets, spaced well apart. Bake in the preheated oven for 10–15 minutes, or until crisp on the outside but soft inside. Let the cookies cool on the baking sheets for 2 minutes, then transfer to wire racks to cool completely.

peanut & coffee cookies

ingredients

makes 14

1 stick butter, softened,
  plus extra for greasing
½ cup firmly packed light
  brown sugar
2 teaspoons coffee extract or
  flavoring
1 teaspoon maple syrup or
  light corn syrup
1⅓ cups all-purpose flour
2 teaspoons baking powder
½ cup coarsely chopped unsalted,
  skinned peanuts

method

1 Preheat the oven to 350°F and grease two large baking sheets.

2 Put the butter and sugar in a bowl and beat together until pale and creamy. Beat in the coffee and maple syrup. Sift in the flour and baking powder, then add the peanuts and mix to form a coarse dough.

3 Divide the dough into 14 even balls and place on the prepared baking sheets, allowing plenty of room for the cookies to spread. Slightly flatten each ball with your fingertips.

4 Bake in the preheated oven for 12–14 minutes, or until just set and pale golden. Let cool on the baking sheets for 5 minutes, then transfer to a wire rack to cool completely. The cookies will become firm as they cool.

cappuccino cookies

ingredients

makes about 30

2 envelopes instant cappuccino
1 tablespoon hot water
2 sticks butter, softened
¾ cup granulated sugar
1 egg yolk, lightly beaten
2¼ cups all-purpose flour
pinch of salt

topping

6 ounces white chocolate,
    broken into pieces
unsweetened cocoa powder,
    for dusting

method

1 Put the instant cappuccino into a small bowl and stir in the hot water to make a paste. Put the butter and sugar in a large bowl and beat together until light and fluffy, then beat in the egg yolk and cappuccino paste. Sift together the flour and salt into the mixture and stir until combined. Halve the dough, shape into balls, wrap in plastic wrap, and chill for 30–60 minutes.

2 Preheat the oven to 375°F. Line two large baking sheets with parchment paper. Unwrap the dough and roll it out between two sheets of parchment paper. Cut out cookies with a 2½-inch circle cutter and place them on the prepared baking sheets, spaced well apart. Bake in the preheated oven for 10–12 minutes, or until golden brown. Let cool for 5–10 minutes, then transfer to wire racks to cool completely.

3 Place the wire racks over a sheet of parchment paper. Put the chocolate in a heatproof bowl, set the bowl over a saucepan of gently simmering water, and heat until melted. Let cool, then spoon the chocolate over the cookies. Let the chocolate set, then dust lightly with cocoa powder.

espresso sugar cookies

ingredients

makes 14

1 stick butter, softened,
   plus extra for greasing
¼ cup granulated sugar
1 teaspoon espresso coffee powder
1 cup all-purpose flour,
   plus extra for dusting
1 tablespoon amber sugar crystals,
   lightly crushed

method

1 Put the butter and sugar in a bowl and beat together until pale and fluffy. Beat in the coffee powder. Sift in the flour and mix to a soft dough. Gather together the dough with your hands and knead gently on a lightly floured surface until smooth. Wrap in plastic wrap and chill in the refrigerator for 1 hour.

2 Preheat the oven to 350°F. Grease two baking sheets.

3 Roll out the dough on a lightly floured surface to a thickness of ¼ inch. Use a 2½-inch circle fluted cutter to stamp out 14 circles, rerolling the dough as necessary. Place on the prepared baking sheets. Sprinkle some sugar crystals in the center of each cookie, pressing down gently.

4 Bake in the preheated oven for 10–14 minutes, or until the cookies are light golden around the edges. Let cool for 5 minutes, then transfer to a wire rack and let cool completely.

chocolate & coffee oatmeal cookies

ingredients

makes 24

1½ sticks butter, plus extra
    for greasing
1 cup firmly packed light
    brown sugar
1 egg
½ cup all-purpose flour, plus extra
    for dusting (optional)
1 teaspoon baking soda
pinch of salt
½ cup whole-wheat flour
1 tablespoon wheat bran
1 cup semisweet
    chocolate chips
2 cups rolled oats
1 tablespoon strong coffee
¾ cup hazelnuts, toasted and
    coarsely chopped

method

1 Preheat the oven to 375°F. Grease two large baking sheets. Put the butter and sugar in a large bowl and beat together until light and fluffy. Add the egg and beat well. Sift the all-purpose flour, baking soda, and salt into another bowl, then add in the whole-wheat flour and bran. Mix in the egg mixture, then stir in the chocolate chips, oats, coffee, and hazelnuts and mix well.

2 Place 24 heaping tablespoons of the dough on the prepared baking sheets, spaced well apart. Alternatively, with lightly floured hands, break off pieces of the dough and roll into 24 balls, place on the baking sheets, then flatten.

3 Bake in the preheated oven for 16–18 minutes, or until golden brown. Let cool for 5 minutes, then transfer to a wire rack to cool completely.

coffee & hazelnut biscotti

ingredients

makes 20

4 tablespoons unsalted butter, plus extra for greasing

1/2 cup granulated sugar

1 egg, beaten

1/3 cup candied peel

1/3 cup blanched hazelnuts

2 teaspoons espresso coffee powder

1 1/3 cups all-purpose flour

1/2 teaspoon baking powder

method

1 Preheat the oven to 350°F. Grease a large baking sheet.

2 Put the butter and sugar in a large bowl and beat together until pale and creamy. Gradually beat in the egg, then stir in the candied peel, hazelnuts, and coffee.

3 Sift in the flour and baking powder and mix to a soft dough. Halve the dough and shape each piece into an 8 x 4-inch rectangle. Place on the prepared baking sheet.

4 Bake in the preheated oven for 20–25 minutes, or until just firm. Do not turn off the oven. Let cool on the baking sheet for 10 minutes, then, using a spatula, transfer each rectangle to a cutting board and cut into ten slices.

5 Place the slices, cut-side down, on the baking sheet. Return to the oven and bake for another 8–10 minutes, or until golden and crisp. Transfer to a wire rack and let cool completely.

family cakes

mocha layer cake

ingredients

serves 8

butter, for greasing
1²/₃ cups all-purpose flour
1 tablespoon baking powder
¹/₄ cup unsweetened
    cocoa powder
¹/₂ cup granulated sugar
2 eggs, beaten
2 tablespoons light corn syrup
²/₃ cup vegetable oil
²/₃ cup milk

filling

1 teaspoon instant coffee
1 tablespoon boiling water
1¹/₄ cups heavy cream
2 tablespoons confectioners' sugar

to decorate

½ cup semisweet chocolate, grated
chocolate curls
confectioners' sugar, for dusting

method

1 Preheat the oven to 350°F. Lightly grease three shallow 7-inch round cake pans. Sift the flour, baking powder, and cocoa into a large bowl, then stir in the sugar. Make a well in the center and stir in the eggs, syrup, oil, and milk. Beat with a wooden spoon, gradually mixing in the dry ingredients to make a smooth batter. Divide the batter among the prepared pans.

2 Bake in the preheated oven for 35–45 minutes, or until springy to the touch. Cool in the pans for 5 minutes, then turn out and cool completely on a wire rack.

3 To make the filling, dissolve the instant coffee in the boiling water and put in a large bowl with the cream and confectioners' sugar. Whip until the cream is just holding its shape, then use half the cream to sandwich together the three cakes. Spread the remaining cream over the top and sides of the cake. Press the grated chocolate into the cream around the side of the cake.

4 Transfer the cake to a serving plate. Lay the chocolate curls over the top of the cake. Cut a few thin strips of parchment paper and place on top of the chocolate curls. Dust lightly with confectioners' sugar to create a striped pattern, then carefully remove the paper. Serve.

coffee & walnut ring

ingredients

serves 10

oil or melted butter,
  for greasing
1⅓ cups all-purpose flour
1 tablespoon baking powder
1½ sticks unsalted butter, softened
¾ cup firmly packed light
  brown sugar
3 eggs, beaten
1 teaspoon coffee extract
½ cup walnut pieces, chopped,
  plus extra walnut halves
  to decorate
¼ cup maple syrup

method

1 Preheat the oven to 325°F. Grease a 1½-quart tube pan, preferably with a nonstick finish.

2 Sift the flour and baking powder into a large bowl and add the butter, sugar, eggs, and coffee. Beat well until the batter is smooth, then stir in the chopped walnuts.

3 Spoon the batter into the prepared pan and smooth the surface with a spatula. Bake in the preheated oven for 40–45 minutes, or until the cake is risen, firm, and golden brown.

4 Let cool in the pan for 10 minutes, then turn out carefully onto a wire rack. While the cake is still warm, spoon half the maple syrup over it. Let cool completely. To serve, top with walnut halves and drizzle with the remaining maple syrup.

gingerbread latte cake

ingredients

serves 10

1½ sticks butter, plus extra
    for greasing
¾ cup firmly packed light
    brown sugar
½ cup light corn syrup
⅓ cup molasses
2 teaspoons instant coffee granules
2¾ cups all-purpose flour
4 teaspoons baking powder
2 teaspoons ground ginger
2 extra-large eggs, beaten

frosting

1 stick butter, softened
3 tablespoons heavy cream
2 teaspoons coffee extract or
    flavoring
1¾ cups confectioners' sugar, sifted
1 tablespoon raw sugar
1 teaspoon instant coffee granules,
    finely ground

method

1 Preheat the oven to 325°F. Grease an 8-inch square cake
    pan and line with parchment paper.

2 Put the butter, sugar, corn syrup, molasses, and coffee
    granules in a small saucepan and heat gently until the
    butter has melted and the sugar has dissolved. Let cool
    for 10 minutes.

3 Sift the flour, baking powder, and ginger into a large
    bowl. Stir in the melted mixture and the eggs and beat
    until smooth and creamy. Spoon the batter into the
    pan and smooth the surface with a spatula.

4 Bake the cake in the preheated oven for 1 hour–
    1 hour 10 minutes, until it is risen, golden brown,
    and a toothpick inserted into the center comes out
    clean. Let cool in the pan for 10 minutes, then turn out
    onto a wire rack to cool completely.

5 To make the frosting, put the butter into a bowl and
    beat with an electric mixer for 2–3 minutes, until pale
    and creamy. Beat in the cream and coffee extract, then
    gradually beat in the confectioners' sugar and continue
    to beat for 2–3 minutes, until light and fluffy.

6 Swirl the frosting over the top of the cake. Mix the
    raw sugar and ground coffee and sprinkle it over
    the frosting.

pecan coffee layer cake

ingredients

serves 10–12

2½ sticks butter, softened,
    plus extra for greasing
2¼ cups all-purpose flour
1 tablespoon baking powder
1⅓ cups granulated sugar
5 eggs, beaten
1 tablespoon instant coffee
    granules, dissolved in
    2 tablespoons hot water
¾ cup pecans, finely ground
chopped pecans, to decorate

frosting

2 cups cream cheese
2 tablespoons maple syrup
1 cup confectioners' sugar

method

1 Preheat the oven to 350°F. Grease three 9-inch round cake pans and line the bottoms with parchment paper.

2 Sift the flour and baking powder into a large bowl. Add the butter, sugar, eggs, and coffee and beat with an electric mixer for 1–2 minutes, until creamy. Fold in the nuts.

3 Divide the batter among the prepared pans and smooth the surfaces with a spatula. Bake in the preheated oven for 20–25 minutes, until risen, golden, and just firm to the touch. Let the cakes cool in the pans for 10 minutes, then turn out onto a wire rack to cool completely.

4 To make the frosting, put the cheese and maple syrup into a bowl and beat together until blended. Sift in the sugar and beat until smooth.

5 Sandwich together the cakes with one-third of the frosting. Spread the remainder over the top and sides of the cake and decorate with chopped pecans.

coffee & walnut cake

ingredients

serves 8

1½ sticks unsalted butter, softened, plus extra for greasing
¾ cup firmly packed light brown sugar
3 extra-large eggs, beaten
3 tablespoons strong black coffee, cooled
1⅓ cups all-purpose flour
3½ teaspoons baking powder
1 cup walnut pieces
walnut halves, to decorate

frosting

1 stick unsalted butter, softened
1⅔ cups confectioners' sugar
1 tablespoon strong black coffee, cooled
½ teaspoon vanilla extract

method

1 Preheat the oven to 350°F. Grease two 8-inch round cake pans and line with parchment paper.

2 Beat together the butter and brown sugar until pale and creamy. Gradually add the eggs, beating well after each addition. Beat in the coffee.

3 Sift the flour and baking powder into the mixture, then fold in lightly and evenly with a metal spoon. Fold in the walnut pieces. Divide the batter between the prepared cake pans and smooth the surfaces with a spatula. Bake in the preheated oven for 20–25 minutes, or until golden brown and springy to the touch. Invert onto a wire rack to cool completely.

4 To make the frosting, beat together the butter, confectioners' sugar, coffee, and vanilla extract, mixing until smooth and creamy.

5 Use about half the frosting to sandwich together the cakes, then spread the remaining frosting on top of the cake and swirl with a spatula. Decorate with walnut halves.

coffee bundt cake

ingredients

serves 14

2½ sticks butter, softened, plus extra for greasing
3¼ cups all-purpose flour, plus extra for dusting
1 tablespoon baking powder
1 teaspoon baking soda
3 tablespoons espresso coffee powder
½ cup firmly packed light brown sugar
1 cup maple syrup
3 eggs, beaten
1 cup buttermilk
1 cup heavy cream

to decorate

¼ cup maple syrup
1⅔ cups confectioners' sugar
1 tablespoon unsalted butter, melted
1½–2 teaspoons water
20 white and dark chocolate-coated coffee beans

method

1 Preheat the oven to 350°F. Grease and lightly flour a 12-cup (standard size) bundt cake pan. Sift the flour, baking powder, baking soda, and coffee powder into a bowl. In a separate bowl, beat together the butter and sugar until pale and creamy. Gradually beat in the maple syrup. Beat in the eggs slowly, adding 3 tablespoons of the flour mixture to prevent the mixture from curdling.

2 Mix the buttermilk and cream and add half to the butter mixture. Sprinkle in half of the flour mixture and fold gently together. Add the remaining buttermilk and flour mixture and mix until just combined.

3 Spoon the batter into the prepared pan and smooth the surface. Bake in the preheated oven for about 50 minutes, or until well risen and a toothpick inserted into the center comes out clean. Let cool in the pan for 10 minutes, then loosen with a knife and turn out onto a wire rack to cool completely.

4 Beat the maple syrup in a bowl with 1¼ cups of the confectioners' sugar and the butter until smooth. Transfer the cake to a serving plate and spoon the icing around the top of the cake so that it runs down the sides. Beat the remaining sugar with the water in a bowl to make a smooth paste. Drizzle the icing over the cake and top with the coffee beans.

coffee fruitcake

ingredients

serves 10

1³⁄₄ cups mixed dried fruit

²⁄₃ cup firmly packed light brown sugar

1¹⁄₄ sticks butter, plus extra for greasing

1 cup strong black coffee

2¹⁄₄ cups all-purpose flour

1 tablespoon baking powder

2 teaspoons allspice

1 extra-large egg, beaten

butter, to serve (optional)

method

1 Put the dried fruit, sugar, butter, and coffee in a large saucepan and heat gently, stirring occasionally, until the butter has melted and the sugar has dissolved. Remove from the heat and let cool for 30 minutes.

2 Preheat the oven to 350°F. Grease a 9-inch loaf pan and line the bottom and the two short sides with a strip of parchment paper.

3 Sift the flour, baking powder, and allspice into a large bowl. Make a well in the center and pour in the fruit and coffee mixture and the beaten egg. Stir until thoroughly mixed.

4 Spoon the cake batter into the prepared pan and smooth the surface. Bake in the preheated oven for 1 hour 15 minutes (covering loosely with aluminum foil after 50 minutes), or until the cake is firm to the touch and a toothpick inserted into the center comes out clean. Let cool in the pan for 10 minutes, then turn out onto a wire rack to cool completely. Serve sliced, spread with butter, if desired.

mocha stollen

ingredients

serves 10

¾ cup milk

4 tablespoons butter

2 teaspoons instant coffee granules

2¾ cups white bread flour,
plus extra for dusting

2 tablespooons packed light
brown sugar

2 teaspoons active dry yeast

2 teaspoons allspice

¼ teaspoon salt

⅓ cup dried sweetened cranberries

¼ cup golden raisins

2 tablespoons candied peel

1 egg, beaten

vegetable oil, for greasing

6 ounces marzipan, rolled into
a 9-inch log shape

confectioners' sugar, to dust

icing

½ cup confectioners' sugar

2 tablespoons unsweetened
cocoa powder

1½–2 tablespoons milk

method

1 Put the milk, butter, and coffee granules in a small saucepan and heat gently until the butter has melted. Let cool for 10 minutes.

2 Sift the flour into a large bowl and stir in the sugar, yeast, allspice, salt, cranberries, golden raisins, and candied peel. Make a well in the center and stir in the milk mixture and egg. Mix to a soft dough, then turn out onto a lightly floured surface and knead for 5–6 minutes, until smooth. Put in a bowl, cover with lightly oiled plastic wrap, and let rest in a warm place for 1½ hours, or until doubled in size. Grease a large baking sheet.

3 Turn out the dough onto a lightly floured surface and lightly knead for 1 minute. Roll out to a 12-inch-long oval. Lay the marzipan down the middle of the dough and fold over the sides to enclose it. Place the stollen, seam-side down, on the prepared baking sheet. Cover with oiled plastic wrap and let rest in a warm place for 40–50 minutes, until doubled in size.

4 Meanwhile, preheat the oven to 375°F. Bake the stollen in the preheated oven for 40–45 minutes, or until golden. Transfer to a wire rack and let cool. Sift the sugar and cocoa powder into a bowl and stir in the milk. Drizzle the icing over the stollen and let set, then dust with confectioners' sugar.

raisin & cinnamon coffee crumb cake

ingredients

serves 10

1½ sticks butter, softened,
   plus extra for greasing
1 cup granulated sugar
3 extra-large eggs, beaten
3 tablespoons strong
   black coffee, cooled
1¾ cups all-purpose flour
2½ teaspoons baking powder
2 teaspoons ground cinnamon
1¼ cups raisins
1 Granny Smith apple, peeled,
   cored, and finely chopped

crumb topping

⅔ cup all-purpose flour
1 teaspoon baking powder
4 tablespoons butter,
   chilled and diced
¼ cup raw sugar
2 teaspoons instant coffee
   granules, finely ground
½ cup chopped mixed nuts
confectioners' sugar, for dusting

method

1 Preheat the oven to 350°F. Grease an 8-inch round springform cake pan and line the bottom with parchment paper.

2 Put the butter and sugar in a large bowl and beat until pale and fluffy, then gradually beat in the eggs and coffee. Sift the flour, baking powder, and cinnamon over the butter-egg mixture, and fold in gently until thoroughly incorporated, then fold in the raisins. Spoon the batter into the prepared pan and sprinkle with the chopped apple.

3 To make the topping, sift the flour and baking powder into a bowl, then add the butter and rub in to make fine crumbs. Stir in the raw sugar, coffee, and nuts. Sprinkle the mixture evenly over the apple.

4 Bake in the preheated oven for 1–1¼ hours, until golden brown, firm to the touch, and a toothpick inserted into the center comes out clean—cover loosely with aluminum foil after about 50 minutes if the crumb topping starts to overbrown. Let cool in the pan for 20 minutes, then unclip the pan and transfer the cake to a wire rack to cool completely. Lightly dust with confectioners' sugar to serve.

banana mocha cake

ingredients

serves 10

1 tablespoon instant
    coffee granules
2 tablespoons water
1 cup firmly packed light
    brown sugar
1¾ sticks butter, softened,
    plus extra for greasing
2¾ cups all-purpose flour,
    plus extra for dusting
3 extra-large eggs, beaten
2 small bananas, peeled
    and mashed
2½ teaspoons baking powder

frosting

3 ounces semisweet chocolate,
    broken into pieces
1 tablespoon unsalted butter
1 tablespoon strong black coffee

method

1 Put the coffee, water, and 2 tablespoons of the sugar
in a small saucepan and heat gently, stirring, until
the coffee and sugar have dissolved. Simmer for
1–2 minutes, until syrupy, then let cool.

2 Preheat the oven to 325°F. Grease and lightly flour a
2½-quart tube cake pan.

3 Put the butter and remaining sugar in a large bowl and
beat together until pale and fluffy. Gradually beat in
the eggs, then the coffee syrup. Stir in the mashed
banana, then sift in the flour and baking powder and
fold in thoroughly.

4 Spoon the batter into the prepared pan and smooth
the surface with a spatula. Bake in the preheated oven
for 45–50 minutes, or until the cake is firm, golden, and
a toothpick inserted into the center comes out clean.
Let cool in the pan for 10 minutes, then turn out onto a
wire rack to cool completely.

5 To make the frosting, put the chocolate, butter, and
coffee in a heatproof bowl set over a saucepan of
simmering water and heat until melted. Remove from
the heat and stir until smooth. Spoon the frosting
over the top of the cake, gently easing it halfway
down the sides. Let set.

espresso sheet cake

ingredients

serves 12

1½ sticks butter, softened, plus extra for greasing
3 tablespoons unsweetened cocoa powder
1 tablespoon espresso coffee powder
¼ cup boiling water
1⅔ cups all-purpose flour
3½ teaspoons baking powder
1 cup granulated sugar
3 eggs
1 teaspoon vanilla extract
1 tablespoon milk

frosting

1 cup mascarpone cheese
¼ cup granulated sugar
1 tablespoon espresso coffee, cooled
¼ cup heavy cream
3 ounces semisweet chocolate, melted

method

1 Preheat the oven to 350°F. Grease a 7 x 11-inch sheet cake pan and line the bottom with parchment paper.

2 Put the cocoa powder, coffee powder, and boiling water in a heatproof bowl and mix together to a smooth paste. Let cool for 10 minutes.

3 Sift the flour and baking powder into a bowl and add the butter, sugar, eggs, vanilla extract, milk, and cocoa mixture. Beat with an electric mixer for 2–3 minutes, until smooth and creamy.

4 Spoon the cake batter into the prepared pan and smooth the surface with a spatula. Bake in the preheated oven for 30–35 minutes, or until risen and just firm to the touch. Let the cake cool in the pan for 10 minutes, then turn out onto a wire rack to cool completely.

5 To make the frosting, put the mascarpone cheese, sugar, coffee, and cream in a bowl and beat together until smooth. Spread over the top of the cake. Spoon the melted chocolate into a paper pastry bag, snip off the end, and pipe thin zigzag lines across the frosting. Let set.

marble cake

ingredients

serves 10

2 sticks butter, softened,
   plus extra for greasing
2 ounces semisweet chocolate,
   broken into pieces
1 tablespoon strong black coffee
2¼ cups all-purpose flour
4 teaspoons baking powder
1 cup granulated sugar
4 eggs, beaten
½ cup almond meal
   (ground almonds)
2 tablespoons milk
1 teaspoon vanilla extract

icing

4 ounces semisweet chocolate,
   broken into pieces
2 tablespoons butter
2 tablespoons water

method

1 Preheat the oven to 350°F and grease a 1¾-quart tube cake pan.

2 Put the chocolate and coffee in a heatproof bowl, set the bowl over a saucepan of gently simmering water, and heat until melted. Let cool.

3 Sift the flour and baking powder into a bowl. Add the butter, sugar, eggs, almond meal, and milk. Beat well until smooth.

4 Transfer half of the batter to a separate bowl and stir in the vanilla extract. Stir the cooled chocolate mixture into the other half of the batter. Place spoonfuls of the two batters alternately into the prepared cake pan, then drag a toothpick through to create a marbled effect. Smooth the surface with a spatula.

5 Bake in the preheated oven for 50–60 minutes, until risen and a toothpick inserted into the cake comes out clean. Let cool in the pan for 5 minutes, then turn out onto a wire rack to cool completely.

6 To make the icing, put the chocolate, butter, and water in a heatproof bowl, set the bowl over a saucepan of gently simmering water and heat until melted. Stir and pour over the top of the cake, working quickly to coat the top and sides. Let set before serving.

spiced coffee & orange swirl cake

ingredients

serves 8–10

1½ sticks butter, softened,
   plus extra for greasing
⅓ cup pecans
¼ cup firmly packed light
   brown sugar
2 teaspoons allspice
1 tablespoon instant coffee powder
1¾ cups all-purpose flour
3½ teaspoons baking powder
1 cup granulated sugar
3 extra-large eggs, beaten
finely grated rind and juice
   of 1 orange

method

1 Preheat the oven to 350°F. Grease an 8-inch round cake pan and line with parchment paper.

2 Put the nuts, brown sugar, allspice, and coffee powder in a food processor or blender and process for a few seconds until finely ground.

3 Sift the flour and baking powder into a large bowl. Add the butter, granulated sugar, eggs, and orange rind and juice and beat with an electric mixer for 1–2 minutes, until smooth and creamy.

4 Spread one-third of the cake batter in the bottom of the prepared pan. Sprinkle over half the nut mixture. Repeat the layers once, then gently spread the remaining cake batter on top. Drag a thin knife through the batter to create a swirled effect.

5 Bake in the preheated oven for 55–65 minutes, or until risen and firm to the touch and a toothpick inserted into the center comes out clean. Let cool in the pan for 10 minutes, then turn out onto a wire rack to cool completely.

mocha-glazed pound cake

ingredients

serves 9

2¼ sticks butter, softened,
    plus extra for greasing
2⅓ cups all-purpose flour
1 teaspoon baking powder
1 cup granulated sugar
1 tablespoon coffee extract
    or flavoring
6 eggs

mocha glaze

4 ounces semisweet chocolate,
    finely chopped
1 tablespoon coffee extract
    or flavoring
1 tablespoon unsalted butter
⅔ cup heavy cream

method

1 Preheat the oven to 350°F. Grease an 8-inch square cake pan and line with parchment paper. Sift the flour and baking powder into a bowl and set aside.

2 Put the butter and sugar in a large bowl and beat with an electric mixer until pale and creamy. Beat in the coffee extract, then beat in the eggs, one at a time, adding a spoonful of the flour mixture after each egg. Fold in the remaining flour. Spoon the batter into the prepared pan and smooth the surface with a spatula.

3 Bake in the preheated oven for 50 minutes–1 hour, or until risen, golden brown, and a toothpick inserted into the center comes out clean. Let cool in the pan for 10 minutes, then turn out the cake onto a wire rack to cool completely.

4 To make the glaze, put the chocolate, coffee extract, and butter in a heatproof bowl. Heat the cream until almost boiling, then pour into the bowl. Stir continuously until the chocolate has melted. Let cool and thicken for about 20 minutes, stirring occasionally. Pour the thick glaze over the cake, allowing it to spill down the sides. Let set before serving.

coffee & walnut swirl

ingredients

serves 6–8

butter, for greasing

3 eggs

1 egg white

½ cup granulated sugar, plus extra
for sprinkling

1 teaspoon coffee extract

½ cup all-purpose flour, sifted

⅓ cup finely chopped walnuts,
plus extra to decorate

filling

¾ cup heavy cream

¼ cup confectioners' sugar, plus
extra for dusting

1 tablespoon coffee liqueur

method

1 Preheat the oven to 400°F. Grease a 13 x 9-inch jelly roll
pan with butter and line with parchment paper.

2 Put the eggs, egg white, and sugar in a heatproof bowl
over a saucepan of hot water. Beat with an electric
mixer until pale and thick enough to leave a trail.

3 Beat in the coffee extract, then lightly fold in the flour
and the finely chopped walnuts with a metal spoon.
Spoon the batter into the prepared pan, spreading
evenly. Bake in the preheated oven for 12–15 minutes,
until golden brown and firm.

4 Sprinkle a sheet of parchment paper with sugar. Turn
out the cake onto the sugar-dusted paper and peel off
the parchment paper from the cooked cake. Trim the
edges. Quickly roll up the cake from one short side,
with the paper inside. Let stand on a wire rack to
cool completely.

5 To make the filling, put the cream, sugar, and liqueur
in a bowl and beat until the mixture begins to hold
its shape.

6 Carefully unroll the cake, remove the paper, and spread
the cream filling over the cake. Roll up carefully. Serve
the roll dusted with confectioners' sugar and decorated
with coarsely chopped walnuts.

chocolate cake with coffee syrup

ingredients

serves 12

1 stick unsalted butter,
    plus extra for greasing
8 ounces semisweet chocolate,
    broken into pieces
1 tablespoon strong black coffee
4 extra-large eggs
2 egg yolks
1/2 cup granulated sugar
1/2 cup all-purpose flour
2 teaspoons ground cinnamon
1/2 cup almond meal
    (ground almonds)
chocolate-covered coffee beans,
    to decorate

syrup

1 1/4 cups strong black coffee
1/2 cup granulated sugar
1 cinnamon stick

method

1 Preheat the oven to 375°F. Grease an 8-inch round cake pan and line the bottom with parchment paper. Put the chocolate, butter, and coffee in a heatproof bowl, set the bowl over a saucepan of gently simmering water, and heat until melted. Stir to blend, then remove from the heat and cool slightly.

2 Put the whole eggs, egg yolks, and sugar in a separate bowl and beat together until thick and pale. Sift the flour and cinnamon over the egg mixture. Add the almonds and the chocolate mixture and fold in carefully. Spoon the batter into the prepared pan and bake in the preheated oven for 35 minutes, or until a toothpick inserted into the center comes out clean. Cool slightly before turning out onto a serving plate.

3 Meanwhile, make the syrup. Put the coffee, sugar, and cinnamon stick in a heavy saucepan and heat gently, stirring, until the sugar has dissolved. Increase the heat and boil for 5 minutes, or until reduced and thickened slightly. Keep warm. Pierce the surface of the cake with a toothpick, then drizzle half the coffee syrup over the cake. Decorate with chocolate-covered coffee beans and serve, cut into wedges, with the remaining coffee syrup.

coffee streusel cake

ingredients

serves 8

1 stick butter, melted and cooled,
    plus extra for greasing
2¼ cups all-purpose flour
1 tablespoon baking powder
⅓ cup granulated sugar
⅔ cup milk
2 eggs
2 tablespoons instant coffee,
    mixed with 1 tablespoon
    boiling water
½ cup chopped almonds
confectioners' sugar, for dusting

topping

⅔ cup all-purpose flour
1 teaspoon baking powder
⅓ cup raw sugar
2 tablespoons butter, diced
1 teaspoon allspice
1 tablespoon water

method

1 Preheat the oven to 375°F. Grease a 9-inch, round springform cake pan and line with parchment paper.

2 Sift the flour and baking powder into a large mixing bowl, then stir in the granulated sugar. In a separate bowl, beat the milk, eggs, melted butter, and coffee mixture and pour onto the dry ingredients. Add the chopped almonds and mix lightly. Spoon the batter into the prepared pan.

3 To make the topping, mix the flour, baking powder, and raw brown sugar. Rub in the butter with your fingertips until the mixture resembles bread crumbs. Sprinkle in the allspice and water and bring the mixture together into loose crumbs. Sprinkle the topping evenly over the surface of the cake batter in the pan.

4 Bake in the preheated oven for about 1 hour, or until a toothpick inserted into the center comes out clean. If the topping starts to brown too quickly, cover loosely with aluminum foil. Let cool in the pan. Turn out, dust with confectioners' sugar, and serve.

sachertorte

ingredients

serves 10

1¼ sticks unsalted butter,
    plus extra for greasing
6 ounces semisweet chocolate,
    broken into pieces
¾ cup granulated sugar
6 eggs, separated
1⅓ cups all-purpose flour

icing

8 ounces semisweet chocolate,
    broken into pieces
5 tablespoons strong black coffee
1⅓ cups confectioners' sugar
⅓ cup apricot preserves, warmed

method

1 Preheat the oven to 300°F. Grease and line a 9-inch round springform cake pan.

2 Put the chocolate in a heatproof bowl, set the bowl over a saucepan of gently simmering water, and heat until melted. In a separate bowl, beat the butter and ⅓ cup of the sugar until pale and fluffy. Add the egg yolks and beat well. Add the chocolate in a thin stream, beating well. Sift in the flour and fold it into the mixture. In a separate bowl, beat the egg whites until they stand in soft peaks. Add the remaining sugar and beat until glossy. Fold half the egg-white mixture into the chocolate mixture, then fold in the remainder.

3 Spoon into the prepared pan and smooth the top. Bake in the preheated oven for 1–1¼ hours, until a toothpick inserted into the center comes out clean. Cool in the pan for 5 minutes, then transfer to a wire rack to cool completely.

4 To make the icing, melt three-quarters of the chocolate and beat in the coffee until smooth. Sift in the sugar and beat. Halve the cake. Spread the preserves over the cut surfaces and sandwich together. Turn out the cake on a wire rack. Spoon the icing over the cake and spread to coat the top and sides. Let set for 5 minutes. Transfer to a serving plate and let set for at least 2 hours.

chocolate truffle torte

ingredients

serves 10

butter, for greasing
¼ cup granulated sugar
2 eggs
2 tablespoons all-purpose flour
¼ cup unsweetened cocoa powder,
    plus extra to decorate
¼ cup strong black coffee, cooled
2 tablespoons brandy

topping

2½ cups heavy whipping cream
16 ounces semisweet chocolate,
    melted and cooled
confectioners' sugar, to decorate

method

1 Preheat the oven to 425°F. Grease a 9-inch springform cake pan and line the bottom with parchment paper. Place the sugar and eggs in a heatproof bowl and set over a saucepan of hot water. Beat together until pale and mousse-like. Sift the flour and cocoa powder into a separate bowl, then fold gently into the cake batter. Pour into the prepared pan and bake in the preheated oven for 7–10 minutes, or until risen and firm to the touch.

2 Transfer to a wire rack to cool. Wash and dry the pan and replace the cooled cake in the pan. Mix the coffee and brandy and brush over the cake.

3 To make the topping, put the cream in a bowl and whip until soft peaks form. Carefully fold in the cooled chocolate. Pour the chocolate mixture over the cake and chill in the refrigerator for 4–5 hours, or until set.

4 To decorate the torte, sift cocoa powder over the top and remove carefully from the pan. Using strips of cardboard or wax paper as a mask, sift bands of confectioners' sugar over the torte to create a striped pattern. To serve, cut into slices with a hot knife.

white chocolate coffee cake

ingredients

serves 8–10

3 tablespoons unsalted butter,
plus extra for greasing
3 ounces white chocolate, broken
into pieces
⅔ cup granulated sugar
4 extra-large eggs, beaten
2 tablespoons strong black coffee
1 teaspoon vanilla extract
1 cup all-purpose flour
white chocolate curls,
to decorate

frosting

6 ounces white chocolate, broken
into pieces
6 tablespoons unsalted butter
½ cup crème fraîche or
cream cheese
1 cup confectioners' sugar, sifted
1 tablespoon coffee liqueur or
strong black coffee

method

1 Preheat the oven to 350°F. Grease two 8-inch cake pans and line the bottoms with parchment paper.

2 Put the butter and chocolate in a heatproof bowl set over a saucepan of hot water and heat on low heat until just melted. Stir, then remove from the heat.

3 Put the granulated sugar, eggs, coffee, and vanilla extract in a large heatproof bowl set over a saucepan of hot water and beat with an electric mixer until the mixture is pale and thick. Remove from the heat, sift in the flour, and fold in lightly. Fold in the butter and chocolate mixture, then divide the batter between the prepared pans. Bake in the preheated oven for 25–30 minutes, until golden brown and springy to the touch. Let cool slightly, then turn out onto a wire rack to cool.

4 To make the frosting, put the chocolate and butter in a heatproof bowl set over a saucepan of hot water and heat gently until melted. Remove from the heat and stir in the crème fraîche, confectioners' sugar, and coffee liqueur. Chill, stirring occasionally, until the mixture is thick and glossy. Sandwich the cakes together with some of the frosting and spread the remainder over the top and sides, swirling with a spatula. Arrange the white chocolate curls over the top and let set.

italian coffee cake

ingredients

serves 8

3 tablespoons butter, melted and
    cooled, plus extra for greasing
4 extra-large eggs
½ cup granulated sugar
1 cup all-purpose flour
unsweetened cocoa powder,
    for dusting
2 ounces semisweet dark
    chocolate, finely grated

espresso syrup

½ cup espresso coffee
½ cup confectioners' sugar

frosting

1 cup mascarpone cheese
⅓ cup granulated sugar
2 tablespoons Marsala wine

method

1 Preheat the oven to 350°F. Grease two 8-inch round
    cake pans and line the bottom with parchment paper.

2 Put the eggs and sugar into a heatproof bowl set over
    a saucepan of simmering water. Beat with an electric
    mixer until the mixture is thick and pale and leaves a
    trail on the surface when the beaters are lifted. Sift in
    the flour and fold in gently. Pour the butter over the
    mixture in a thin stream and fold in until incorporated.

3 Divide the batter between the prepared pans and bake
    in the preheated oven for 20–25 minutes, until light
    golden and springy to the touch. Let cool in the pans
    for 5 minutes, then invert onto a wire rack.

4 To make the syrup, put the coffee and sugar in a small
    saucepan and bring to a boil. Simmer for 3–4 minutes,
    until syrupy. Let cool for 10 minutes. Pierce the tops of
    the warm cakes all over with a toothpick and spoon
    over the coffee syrup. Let cool completely.

5 To make the frosting, put all the ingredients into a
    bowl and beat together until smooth. Spread half the
    frosting over one cake and sprinkle with half the grated
    chocolate. Top with the second cake and swirl the
    remaining frosting over the top. Dust with the cocoa
    powder and sprinkle with the chocolate.

mocha cake

ingredients

serves 12

2 sticks butter, softened, plus extra for greasing
1¾ cups self-rising flour
3½ teaspoons baking powder
2 tablespoons unsweetened cocoa powder
1 cup firmly packed light brown sugar
4 extra-large eggs, beaten
4 ounces semisweet chocolate, melted
2 tablespoons granulated sugar
3 tablespoons strong black coffee

frosting

6 tablespoons unsalted butter, softened
1 cup mascarpone cheese
½ cup confectioners' sugar
2 tablespoons strong black coffee, cooled
unsweetened cocoa powder, for dusting
chocolate-coated coffee beans, to decorate

method

1 Preheat the oven to 350°F. Grease two 8-inch cake pans and line the bottom with parchment paper.

2 Sift the flour, baking powder, and cocoa powder into a large bowl. Add the butter, brown sugar, and eggs and, using an electric mixer, beat together for 3–4 minutes, or until the mixture is smooth and creamy. Fold in the melted chocolate.

3 Divide the batter between the prepared cake pans and bake in the preheated oven for 25–30 minutes, or until risen and firm to the touch.

4 Put the granulated sugar and black coffee in a small saucepan and heat gently for 1–2 minutes. Let cool for 10 minutes. Pierce the tops of the warm cakes all over with a toothpick and spoon the coffee syrup over the cakes. Let the cakes cool completely in the pans.

5 To make the frosting, put the butter and mascarpone cheese in a bowl and beat together until well blended. Beat in the confectioners' sugar and coffee until smooth.

6 Remove the cakes from the pans and sandwich together with half the frosting. Swirl the remaining frosting over the top of the cake. Dust with cocoa powder and decorate with chocolate-coated coffee beans.

coffee & amaretto cream cake

ingredients

serves 8

1½ sticks butter, softened,
    plus extra for greasing
1⅓ cups all-purpose flour
1 tablespoon baking powder
¾ cup firmly packed light
    brown sugar
3 eggs, beaten
3 tablespoons strong black
    coffee, cooled
2 ounces semisweet chocolate,
    melted, and
    1 tablespoon toasted slivered
    almonds, to decorate

filling

2 cups heavy cream
2–3 tablespoons amaretto

method

1 Preheat the oven to 350°F. Grease two 8-inch round cake pans and line the bottom with parchment paper.

2 Sift the flour and baking powder into a bowl and add the butter, sugar, eggs, and coffee. Beat with an electric mixer for 1–2 minutes, until smooth and creamy. Divide the batter between the prepared pans and smooth the surface with a spatula.

3 Bake in the preheated oven for 25–30 minutes, or until golden brown and springy to the touch. Let cool in the pans for 5 minutes, then turn out the cakes onto a wire rack to cool completely.

4 To make the filling, put the cream into a bowl with the amaretto and whip until it holds soft peaks. Sandwich the cakes together with half the cream and spread the remainder over the top. Spoon the melted chocolate into a paper pastry bag and snip off the end. Pipe swirls of chocolate on the top of the cake and sprinkle with the slivered almonds.

desserts & other treats

coffee ice cream

ingredients

serves 6

1 ounce semisweet chocolate, plus extra to decorate
1 cup ricotta cheese
⅓ cup low-fat plain yogurt
⅓ cup granulated sugar
¼ cup strong black coffee, cooled
½ teaspoon ground cinnamon
dash of vanilla extract

method

1 Grate the chocolate and set aside. Put the ricotta cheese, yogurt, and sugar in a food processor or blender and process until smooth. Transfer to a large bowl and beat in the coffee, cinnamon, vanilla extract, and grated chocolate.

2 Spoon the mixture into a freezerproof container and freeze for 1½ hours, or until slushy. Remove from the freezer, turn into a bowl, and beat. Return to the container and freeze for 1½ hours.

3 Repeat this beating and freezing process two more times. Keep in the freezer until 15 minutes before serving, then transfer to the refrigerator to soften slightly before serving. Serve in scoops, decorated with a little grated chocolate.

cappuccino ice cream

ingredients

serves 4

²/₃ cup whole milk
2½ cups heavy whipping cream
¼ cup finely ground fresh coffee
3 extra-large egg yolks
½ cup granulated sugar
unsweetened cocoa powder,
    for dusting
chocolate-coated coffee beans,
    to decorate

method

1 Pour the milk and 2 cups of the cream into a heavy saucepan, stir in the coffee, and bring almost to a boil. Remove from the heat, let steep for 5 minutes, then strain through a paper coffee filter or a strainer lined with cheesecloth.

2 Put the egg yolks and sugar in a large bowl and beat together until pale and the mixture leaves a trail when the beaters are lifted. Slowly add the milk mixture, stirring all the time with a wooden spoon. Strain the mixture into the rinsed-out pan or a double boiler and cook over low heat for 10–15 minutes, stirring all the time, until the mixture thickens enough to coat the back of the spoon. Do not let the mixture boil or it will curdle. Remove from the heat and let cool for at least 1 hour, stirring from time to time to prevent a skin from forming.

3 Churn the cold custard in an ice-cream maker, following the manufacturer's directions.

4 To serve, whip the remaining cream until it holds soft peaks. Scoop the ice cream into wide-brimmed coffee cups and smooth the tops. Spoon the whipped cream over the top of each and sprinkle with cocoa powder. Decorate with chocolate-coated coffee beans.

brown sugar mocha cream

ingredients

serves 4–6

1¼ cups heavy cream
1 teaspoon vanilla extract
2 cups fresh whole-wheat
    bread crumbs
⅓ cup firmly packed dark
    brown sugar
1 tablespoon instant
    coffee granules
2 tablespoons unsweetened
    cocoa powder
grated chocolate, to decorate
    (optional)

method

1 Whip the cream and vanilla extract in a large bowl until it is thick and holds soft peaks.

2 Mix the bread crumbs, sugar, coffee, and cocoa powder in another large bowl and layer the dry mixture with the whipped cream in serving glasses, ending with whipped cream. Sprinkle with grated chocolate, if using.

3 Cover and let chill in the refrigerator for several hours, or overnight.

cappuccino mousses

ingredients

serves 4

1 sheet gelatin

2 tablespoons instant
   coffee granules

¼ cup water

⅓ cup superfine sugar or
   granulated sugar

1¾ cups heavy cream

1 extra-large egg white

1 tablespoon finely grated
   milk chocolate

4 chocolate-coated coffee beans,
   to decorate

method

1 Soak the gelatin in a bowl of cold water for 5 minutes,
   until soft. Put the coffee granules, water, and
   2 tablespoons of the sugar into a small saucepan
   and heat gently until the coffee has dissolved.

2 Drain the softened gelatin, squeezing out any excess
   water, and add to the hot coffee. Stir gently, until the
   gelatin has dissolved, then let the mixture cool for
   20 minutes.

3 Pour the cream into a bowl and whip until it holds soft
   peaks. Remove ⅓ cup of the cream and reserve for
   decoration. Gently fold the coffee mixture into the
   remaining cream.

4 Beat the egg white in a clean, grease-free bowl until it
   forms soft peaks, then beat in the remaining sugar.
   Fold into the coffee cream and divide the mixture
   among four dessert glasses. Spoon the reserved
   whipped cream on top of the mousses.

5 Chill in the refrigerator for 1–2 hours, or until set.
   Sprinkle with the grated chocolate and decorate
   each mousse with a chocolate-coated coffee bean.

white chocolate tiramisu

ingredients

serves 4

16 ladyfingers
1 cup strong black coffee,
    cooled to room temperature
1/4 cup almond-flavored liqueur,
    such as amaretto
1 cup mascarpone cheese
1 1/4 cups heavy cream
3 tablespoons granulated sugar
4 ounces white chocolate, grated
1/4 cup toasted slivered almonds,
    to decorate

method

1 Break the ladyfingers into pieces and divide half of them equally among four serving glasses. Mix together the coffee and liqueur in a small bowl, then pour half the mixture over the ladyfingers in the glasses.

2 Beat the mascarpone, cream, sugar, and half of the chocolate in a bowl. Spread half the mixture over the coffee-soaked ladyfingers, then arrange the remaining ladyfingers on top. Pour the rest of the coffee mixture over the top layer, then spread with the remaining cream mixture. Sprinkle with the remaining chocolate.

3 Cover with plastic wrap and chill for at least 2 hours, or until required. Sprinkle with the slivered almonds before serving.

espresso crème brûlée

ingredients

serves 4

2 cups heavy cream

1 tablespoon instant espresso powder

4 extra-large egg yolks

¾ cup granulated sugar, plus extra for sprinkling

2 tablespoons coffee liqueur, such as Kahlúa

method

1 Preheat the oven to 225°F and put four shallow ovenproof white porcelain dishes on a baking sheet.

2 Put the cream in a small saucepan over medium-high heat and heat until small bubbles appear around the edges. Mix in the espresso powder, stirring until it dissolves, then remove the pan from the heat and let stand until completely cool.

3 Lightly beat the egg yolks in a bowl, then add the sugar and continue beating until thick and creamy.

4 Reheat the cream over medium-high heat until small bubbles appear around the edges. Stir the hot cream into the egg-yolk mixture, beating continuously. Stir in the coffee liqueur. Divide the custard mixture among the dishes and bake for 35–40 minutes, or until the custard wobbles slightly when you shake the dishes.

5 Remove the custards from the oven and let cool completely. Cover with plastic wrap and let chill in the refrigerator for at least 4 hours, but ideally overnight.

6 Before you are ready to serve, preheat the broiler to high. Sprinkle each custard with the sugar and put the dishes under the preheated broiler until the topping is golden and bubbling. Let cool for a few minutes before serving.

hot chocolate soufflé with coffee zabaglione

ingredients

serves 4–6

butter, for greasing
¼ cup granulated sugar,
    plus extra for coating
3 tablespoons cornstarch
1 cup milk
4 ounces semisweet chocolate,
    broken into pieces
4 eggs, separated
confectioners' sugar, for dusting

zabaglione

2 eggs, beaten
3 egg yolks
⅓ cup granulated sugar
4 teaspoons instant coffee granules
2 tablespoons brandy

method

1 Preheat the oven to 375°F. Grease a 1-quart soufflé dish and coat with granulated sugar. To make the soufflé, put the cornstarch in a bowl. Add a little milk and stir until smooth. Pour the remaining milk into a heavy saucepan and add the chocolate. Heat gently until the chocolate has melted, then stir. Pour the chocolate milk onto the cornstarch paste, stirring. Return to the pan and bring to a boil, stirring. Simmer for 1 minute. Remove from the heat and stir in the egg yolks, one at a time. Cover and cool slightly.

2 Put the egg whites in a large, clean bowl and beat until soft peaks form. Gradually beat in the granulated sugar until stiff but not dry. Stir a little of the egg whites into the chocolate mixture, then carefully fold in the remainder. Pour into the prepared soufflé dish, then bake in the preheated oven for 40 minutes, or until it is well risen and wobbles slightly when shaken.

3 Just before the soufflé is ready, make the coffee zabaglione. Put all the ingredients in a heavy saucepan over low heat and cook, beating continuously, until the mixture is thick and light. Dust a little confectioners' sugar over the soufflé and serve immediately, with the zabaglione.

irish cream cheesecake

ingredients

serves 8

vegetable oil, for oiling
6 ounces chocolate-chip cookies
4 tablespoons unsalted butter
crème fraîche or Greek-style yogurt
   and fresh strawberries, to serve

filling

8 ounces semisweet chocolate,
   broken into pieces
8 ounces milk chocolate,
   broken into pieces
1/4 cup granulated sugar
1 1/2 cups cream cheese
2 cups heavy cream,
   lightly whipped
2 tablespoons Irish cream liqueur
1 tablespooon strong black coffee

method

1 Line the bottom of an 8-inch round springform cake pan with parchment paper and brush the sides with oil. Put the cookies in a plastic food bag and crush with a rolling pin. Put the butter in a saucepan and heat gently until melted. Stir in the crushed cookies. Press into the bottom of the prepared cake pan and chill in the refrigerator for 1 hour.

2 Put the semisweet chocolate and milk chocolate into a heatproof bowl, set the bowl over a saucepan of gently simmering water, and heat until melted. Cool. Put the sugar and cream cheese in a bowl and beat until smooth, then fold in the cream. Fold the melted chocolate into the cream-cheese mixture, then stir in the liqueur.

3 Spoon into the cake pan and smooth the surface with a spatula. Let chill in the refrigerator for 2 hours, or until firm. Transfer to a serving plate and cut into slices. Serve with crème fraîche and sliced strawberries.

caramel coffee meringue

ingredients

serves 10

4 extra-large egg whites
1 cup granulated sugar
1 teaspoon vanilla extract
1 teaspoon white-wine vinegar
1 teaspoon cornstarch
2 teaspoons instant coffee
   granules, finely ground
2 tablespoons chopped hazelnuts

filling

2 cups heavy cream
2 teaspoons coffee extract
   or flavoring
1/3 cup dulce de leche
   (caramel sauce)
1 ounce semisweet chocolate,
   finely grated

method

1 Preheat the oven to 275°F. Line a large baking sheet with parchment paper and mark with a 9-inch circle.

2 Put the egg whites in a clean, grease-free bowl and beat until they hold stiff peaks. Gradually beat in the sugar, 1 tablespoon at a time, until all the sugar has been incorporated and the meringue is firm and glossy. Mix the vanilla extract, vinegar, and cornstarch and fold into the meringue with the coffee granules.

3 Spoon the meringue into the circle on the lined baking sheet. Make a dip in the center and swirl and peak the meringue with the back of a spoon. Sprinkle with the chopped hazelnuts.

4 Bake in the preheated oven for 1–1¼ hours, or until crisp on the outside. Turn off the oven and let the meringue cool in the oven for at least 2 hours or overnight (don't worry if it cracks a little on cooling).

5 To make the filling, put the cream into a bowl with the coffee extract and whip until it holds soft peaks. Gently fold the dulce de leche through the cream to create a rippled effect. Spoon the cream on top of the meringue and sprinkle with the grated chocolate.

mocha creams

ingredients

serves 2–4

12 marshmallows
1/2 cup strong black coffee
2 ounces semisweet chocolate,
    finely chopped
    or grated
1 1/4 cups heavy cream

method

1 Put the marshmallows in a saucepan with the coffee and half the chocolate. Heat gently until melted. Remove the pan from the heat and allow to cool.

2 Whip the cream in a large bowl until thick and holding soft peaks, then gently stir in the coffee mixture.

3 Spoon into two to four serving bowls or dishes and sprinkle with the remaining chocolate. Chill in the refrigerator until ready to serve.

mocha fondue

ingredients

serves 4

8 ounces semisweet chocolate (at least 50 percent cocoa solids), broken into small pieces
½ cup heavy cream
1 tablespoon instant coffee granules
3 tablespoons coffee-flavored liqueur, such as Kahlúa

for the dippers

small sweet cookies, such as amaretti
plain or coffee-flavored marble cake or sponge cake, cut into bite-size pieces
whole seedless grapes
firm peaches or nectarines, pitted and sliced

method

1 Arrange the dippers decoratively on a serving platter or individual serving plates and set aside.

2 Put the chocolate in a heatproof bowl and set the bowl over a saucepan of gently simmering water, making sure that the bowl does not touch the water. Add the cream and coffee granules and heat, stirring, until melted and smooth. Remove from the heat and stir in the liqueur, then carefully pour the chocolate mixture into a warm fondue pot.

3 Using protective gloves, transfer the fondue pot to a lit tabletop burner. To serve, instruct your guests to spear the dippers with fondue forks and dip them into the fondue.

mochachino brownies

ingredients

makes 8–9

1 stick unsalted butter, plus extra
for greasing
4 ounces semisweet chocolate,
broken into pieces
2 tablespoons strong black coffee
1¼ cups granulated sugar
½ teaspoon ground cinnamon
3 eggs, beaten
⅔ cup all-purpose flour
⅓ cup milk chocolate chips
½ cup toasted walnuts, skinned
and chopped, plus extra
to decorate

white mocha sauce

½ cup heavy cream
3 ounces white chocolate,
broken into pieces
1 tablespoon strong black coffee

method

1 Preheat the oven to 350°F. Grease and line a 9-inch
square baking pan.

2 Put the butter, chocolate. and coffee in a medium
saucepan over low heat and stir until just melted and
smooth. Cool slightly.

3 Beat in the sugar, cinnamon, and eggs. Beat in the flour,
chocolate chips, and walnuts. Pour the batter into the
prepared pan.

4 Bake in the oven for 30–35 minutes, until just firm but
still moist inside. Cool in the pan, then cut into squares
or bars.

5 Meanwhile, make the sauce by putting all the
ingredients in a small saucepan over low heat,
stirring occasionally, until melted and smooth.

6 Put the brownies on individual plates and spoon the
warm sauce on top. Decorate with chopped walnuts
and serve.

raspberry dessert cake

ingredients

serves 8–10

2 sticks unsalted butter,
 plus extra for greasing
8 ounces semisweet chocolate,
 broken into pieces
1 tablespoon strong dark coffee
5 eggs
1/2 cup granulated sugar
1/2 cup all-purpose flour
1 teaspoon ground cinnamon
1 1/2 cups fresh raspberries,
 plus extra to serve
confectioners' sugar, for dusting
whipped cream, to serve

method

1 Preheat the oven to 325°F. Grease a 9-inch cake pan and line the bottom with parchment paper. Put the chocolate, butter, and coffee in a heatproof bowl, set the bowl over a saucepan of gently simmering water, and heat until melted. Remove from the heat and stir, then allow to cool slightly.

2 Beat the eggs and sugar in a separate bowl until pale and thick. Gently fold the chocolate mixture into the egg and sugar mixture.

3 Sift the flour and cinnamon into another bowl, then fold into the chocolate mixture. Pour into the prepared pan and sprinkle the raspberries evenly over the top.

4 Bake in the preheated oven for about 35–45 minutes, or until the cake is well risen and springy to the touch. Allow to cool in the pan for 15 minutes before turning out onto a large serving plate. Dust with confectioners' sugar before serving with fresh raspberries and whipped cream.

mocha coconut clusters

ingredients

makes 30

4 ounces milk chocolate,
    broken into small pieces
2 tablespoons butter
1 teaspoon instant coffee granules
½ cup shredded unsweetened
    dried coconut

method

1 Line two to three baking sheets with parchment paper. Put the chocolate and butter in a heatproof bowl, set the bowl over a saucepan of gently simmering water, and heat, stirring, until melted and smooth. Remove the bowl from the heat.

2 Stir the coffee granules into the chocolate until dissolved, then stir in the coconut.

3 Put heaping teaspoons of the mixture on the prepared baking sheets, cover, and chill in the refrigerator until set. To serve, put each cluster in a paper candy cup.

mocha pecan tarts

ingredients

serves 4

1 cup all-purpose flour,
    plus extra for dusting
6 tablespoons unsalted butter,
    chilled and diced
2 tablespoons confectioners' sugar
1 egg yolk

filling

1/4 cup firmly packed light
    brown sugar
4 tablespoons butter
1 1/2 teaspoons instant
    coffee granules
2 ounces semisweet chocolate,
    finely chopped
3 tablespoons maple syrup
2 tablespoons light corn syrup
2 extra-large eggs, beaten
1 cup pecans

method

1 Put the flour, butter, and confectioners' sugar into a food processor or blender. Process for a few seconds to make fine crumbs. With the machine running, add the egg yolk and process until the mixture begins to bind together. Turn out onto a lightly floured surface and knead gently until smooth. Wrap in plastic wrap and chill in the refrigerator for 30 minutes.

2 Divide the dough into four pieces. Roll out on a lightly floured surface and use to line four 4-inch loose-bottomed fluted mini tart pans. Prick the bottoms with a fork and chill for 1 hour. Meanwhile, preheat the oven to 375°F. Place a baking sheet in the oven.

3 To make the filling, put the sugar, butter, and coffee granules into a small saucepan and heat gently, stirring, until the sugar and coffee have dissolved. Remove from the heat, add the chocolate, and stir until melted. Let cool for 5 minutes, then beat in the maple syrup, corn syrup, and eggs.

4 Chop two-thirds of the nuts and stir into the mixture. Divide the mixture among the pastry shells and top with the remaining nuts. Place the tarts on the preheated baking sheet and bake for 20–25 minutes, or until the pastry is golden and the filling has just set. Serve warm or cold.

hot espresso cakes

ingredients

serves 6

oil or melted butter, for greasing
1⅓ cups all-purpose flour
1 tablespoon baking powder
1 tablespoon unsweetened
    cocoa powder
1½ sticks unsalted butter, softened
¾ cup firmly packed light
    brown sugar
3 eggs, beaten
1 teaspoon vanilla extract
3 tablespoons strong espresso
    coffee, cooled
brown sugar crystals, to serve

sauce

1 tablespoon cornstarch
1 cup strong espresso coffee
½ cup light cream
3 tablespoons packed light
    brown sugar

method

1 Preheat the oven to 350°F. Grease and line a 7 x 11-inch rectangular cake pan.

2 Sift the flour, baking powder, and cocoa into a large bowl and add the butter, sugar, eggs, and vanilla extract. Beat well until the batter is smooth, then beat in the coffee.

3 Spoon the batter into the prepared pan and smooth the surface with a spatula. Bake in the preheated oven for 30–35 minutes, or until the cake has risen and is firm and golden brown.

4 Meanwhile, to make the sauce, mix the cornstarch with 2 tablespoons of the coffee, then add to a saucepan with the remaining coffee, the cream, and sugar. Heat gently, stirring, until boiling, then reduce the heat and stir for 2 minutes, or until slightly thickened.

5 Using a 3½-inch plain cookie cutter, stamp out six circles from the cake (trimmings can be eaten cold). Place on warm serving plates, spoon the sauce over the top, and sprinkle each with a few sugar crystals.

espresso mint chocolate truffles

ingredients

makes 24

8 ounces semisweet chocolate,
   broken into pieces
4 tablespoons unsalted butter
2/3 cup heavy cream
2 tablespoons espresso
   coffee, cooled
few drops peppermint extract
1–2 tablespoons unsweetened
   cocoa powder

method

1 Put the chocolate and butter into a heatproof bowl, set the bowl over a saucepan of gently simmering water, and heat until melted. Remove from the heat and stir until smooth. Cool for 5 minutes.

2 Mix the cream, coffee, and peppermint extract and stir into the chocolate mixture. Cool for 20–30 minutes, stirring occasionally, then chill in the refrigerator for 2–3 hours, until firm enough to shape.

3 Sift the cocoa powder onto a flat plate. Divide and shape the chocolate mixture into 24 truffles, rolling lightly between the palms of your hands. Roll each truffle in cocoa powder to coat. Chill in the refrigerator for 1–2 hours, until firm.

variation

For a delicious nutty coating, roll the truffles in 1 cup of finely chopped walnuts, pecans, or pistachios instead of cocoa powder.

savory recipes

coffee-braised beef pot roast

ingredients

serves 4

2¾-pound beef brisket
salt and pepper
1 tablespoon butter
2 tablespoons sunflower oil
2 onions, cut into wedges
5 carrots, cut into chunks
2 parsnips, cut into chunks
1¼ cups strong black coffee, cooled
1 cup beef stock
2 tablespoons tomato paste
2 tablespoons Worcestershire sauce
1 tablespoon balsamic vinegar
few fresh thyme sprigs,
    plus extra to garnish
2 tablespoons cornstarch
2–3 tablespoons water
boiled potatoes, to serve

method

1 Preheat the oven to 325°F. Season the beef with salt and pepper.

2 Heat half the butter and half the oil in a large skillet. Add the beef and cook over high heat for a few minutes, until browned all over. Transfer to a large casserole dish or Dutch oven.

3 Add the remaining butter and oil to the skillet, then add the onions, carrots, and parsnips and sauté for 5 minutes. Stir in the coffee, stock, tomato paste, Worcestershire sauce, and vinegar and bring to a boil.

4 Spoon the vegetables and liquid around the beef. Lightly season with salt and pepper and add the thyme. Cover and cook in the preheated oven for 2¼ hours.

5 Remove the casserole from the oven. Blend the cornstarch to a paste with the water and stir into the hot liquid. Return the casserole to the oven, cover, and cook for an additional 30–40 minutes, until the beef and vegetables are tender and the liquid has thickened.

6 Remove the beef from the casserole dish and carve into thick slices. Divide the vegetables and gravy among four shallow serving bowls, top with the beef, and garnish with thyme sprigs. Serve with boiled potatoes.

blackened coffee rib-eye steaks

ingredients

serves 2

2 teaspoons finely ground espresso coffee

2 teaspoons dried oregano

1 teaspoon packed light brown sugar

1 teaspoon pepper

1/2 teaspoon sea salt

2 rib-eye steaks (at room temperature), each about 8 ounces and about 1 inch thick

1 tablespoon olive oil

2 tablespoons butter

arugula and watercress salad, to serve

fresh Parmesan cheese shavings, to garnish

method

1 Mix the coffee, oregano, sugar, pepper, and salt and spread on a shallow plate. Dip each side of the steaks in the mixture to coat.

2 Heat the oil and butter in a large, heavy skillet until sizzling. Add the steaks and cook on each side for 2–3 minutes, until black on the outside for medium-rare. Increase the cooking time slightly for well-done steaks.

3 Transfer the steaks to a warm plate. Cover with aluminum foil and allow to rest in a warm place for 10 minutes.

4 To serve, slice each steak into five to six slices and place on warm serving plates. Pour any meat juices over the steak and serve with an arugula and watercress salad, garnished with Parmesan cheese shavings.

beef in coffee sauce

ingredients

serves 6

¼ cup sunflower oil
3 pounds eye of round steak
   or chuck steak, cut into
   1-inch cubes
4 onions, sliced
1 garlic clove, finely chopped
⅓ cup all-purpose flour
1¼ cups red wine
pinch of dried oregano
1 small fresh rosemary sprig
2 cups black coffee
salt and pepper
fresh marjoram sprigs, to garnish
mashed sweet potatoes, to serve

method

1 Heat the oil in a large, deep skillet. Add the steak cubes and cook over medium heat, stirring frequently, for 8–10 minutes, until evenly browned. Using a slotted spoon, transfer to a casserole dish. Preheat the oven to 325°F.

2 Add the onions and garlic to the skillet, reduce the heat, and cook, stirring occasionally, for 10 minutes, until softened and just beginning to brown. Stir in the flour and cook, stirring continuously, for 1 minute. Gradually stir in the wine, a little at a time. Add the oregano and rosemary, season with salt and pepper, pour in the coffee, and bring to a boil, stirring continuously.

3 Transfer the mixture to the casserole dish. Cover and cook in the preheated oven for 2–2¼ hours, until the meat is tender. Remove and discard the rosemary sprig. Taste and adjust the seasoning, adding salt and pepper, if needed. Garnish with marjoram sprigs and serve immediately with mashed sweet potatoes.

cowboy coffee burgers

ingredients

serves 4

1 tablespoon instant coffee granules, finely ground
2 teaspoons packed light brown sugar
1 teaspoon salt
1/4 teaspoon pepper
1 pound ground chuck beef
1 small onion, grated
1 egg yolk
olive oil, for brushing

to serve

4 hamburger buns
1/4 cup mayonnaise
1 teaspoon smooth mustard
peppery salad greens
4 beefsteak tomato slices

method

1 Put the coffee, sugar, salt, and pepper into a large bowl and mix. Add the beef, onion, and egg yolk and mix with your hands until thoroughly combined. Divide the mixture into four portions and shape each into a patty.

2 Preheat a ridged grill pan or cast-iron skillet. Lightly brush the patties with oil and cook for 6–8 minutes on each side, or until cooked through. Alternatively, cook under a hot broiler.

3 To serve, halve and lightly toast the burger buns. Mix the mayonnaise and mustard. Put some salad greens, a tomato slice, and a burger on top of four bun halves. Add a dollop of mustard-mayonnaise and top with the remaining bun halves. Serve immediately.

coffee barbecue-glazed spareribs

ingredients

serves 4

2 racks pork spareribs,
about 1¾ pounds
3 tablespoons instant coffee
granules, dissolved in
⅓ cup hot water
⅓ cup ketchup
2 tablespoons vegetable oil
3 tablespoons Worcestershire sauce
3 tablespoons smooth
mango chutney
salt and pepper
salad, to serve

method

1 Put the racks of ribs into a large saucepan and cover with water. Bring to a boil, skim off any scum from the surface, then simmer for 25 minutes.

2 Lift the ribs out of the water and place on a metal rack set over a large roasting pan. Preheat the oven to 375°F.

3 Put the coffee, ketchup, oil, Worcestershire sauce, and chutney into a bowl and mix together. Season with salt and pepper.

4 Liberally brush the coffee glaze over the racks of ribs. Roast in the preheated oven for 45 minutes, basting occasionally, until the glaze is sticky and lightly charred in places and the ribs are tender. Serve immediately with salad.

coffee-glazed ham

ingredients

serves 10

4½-pound Virginia or other
    country ham
1 onion, quartered
few black peppercorns
1 bay leaf
½ cup cold strong black coffee
½ cup raw brown sugar
⅓ cup honey
2 tablespoons whole-grain
    mustard
1 tablespoon white-wine vinegar
bay leaves, to garnish

method

1 Put the ham into a large, deep saucepan and cover with cold water. Add the onion, peppercorns, and bay leaf and bring to a boil. Reduce the heat to simmering, cover, and cook for 1½ hours. Add more boiling water, if needed.

2 Meanwhile, put the coffee, sugar, honey, mustard, and vinegar into a small saucepan. Bring to a boil, then simmer for 10–15 minutes, until syrupy. Set aside.

3 Remove the ham from the liquid and allow to cool for 10 minutes, then cut away the skin, leaving a thin layer of fat. Score the fat into diamonds with the tip of a knife. Line a roasting pan with aluminum foil and place the ham in the pan. Preheat the oven to 350°F.

4 Pour two-thirds of the coffee glaze over the ham. Roast in the preheated oven for 25 minutes, then pour the remaining glaze over the ham. Roast for an additional 35–45 minutes, basting 2–3 times, until the glaze is dark golden and caramelized at the edges.

5 Cover the ham and rest it in a warm place for 15 minutes before carving. Pour all the juices from the lined roasting pan into a small pitcher. Garnish the ham with the bay leaves and serve with the juice.

coffee-crusted lamb cutlets

ingredients

serves 2

3 garlic cloves, crushed
1 tablespoon instant coffee granules
2 teaspoons pepper
½ teaspoon sea salt
2 thick lamb cutlets, about 6 ounces each
1 tablespoon sunflower oil
mint sprigs, to garnish

to serve

sautéed or boiled new potatoes
fresh, cooked peas and beans

method

1 Grind the crushed garlic, coffee, pepper, and salt into a coarse paste using a mortar and pestle. Spread the paste over both sides of each lamb cutlet. Place on a plate, cover, and let marinate in the refrigerator for 1–2 hours.

2 Preheat the oven to 400°F.

3 Heat the oil in a skillet until almost smoking. Add the meat and sear in the hot oil, turning, until browned all over.

4 Transfer to a shallow roasting pan and cook in the preheated oven for 15–20 minutes, depending on the thickness of the cutlets and how well done you would like the meat. Remove from the oven, cover with aluminum foil, and allow to rest in a warm place for 10 minutes.

5 Thickly slice each cutlet and arrange on warm serving plates. Garnish with mint and serve immediately with potatoes and freshly cooked peas and beans.

coffee-marinated chicken drumsticks

ingredients

serves 4

8 large chicken drumsticks
⅔ cup strong black coffee, cooled
3 tablespoons honey
3 tablespoons sweet chili sauce
1 tablespoon dark soy sauce
salt and pepper
fries and oven-roasted tomatoes
    on the vine, to serve

method

1 Place the drumsticks in a shallow, nonmetallic dish. Mix the coffee, honey, chili sauce, and soy sauce and pour the marinade over the drumsticks.

2 Lightly season with salt and pepper, cover, and marinate at room temperature for 1–2 hours.

3 Preheat the oven to 400°F. Remove the drumsticks from the marinade and place in a roasting pan. Roast in the preheated oven for 20 minutes. Meanwhile, pour the marinade into a small saucepan, bring to a boil, then reduce the heat and simmer gently for 15 minutes, until syrupy.

4 Remove the pan from the oven and pour the hot marinade all over the drumsticks. Return to the oven and roast, basting occasionally, for an additional 20–25 minutes, or until they are cooked through and golden brown. Serve hot or cold with fries and oven-roasted tomatoes on the vine.

turkey stir-fry with spiced coffee glaze

ingredients

serves 4

1 pound turkey breast, sliced into thin strips
1 teaspoon finely grated fresh ginger
2 garlic cloves, crushed
1 teaspoon five-spice seasoning
4 teaspoons sesame oil
¼ cup strong black coffee, cooled
¼ cup teriyaki sauce
2 tablespoons honey
2 tablespoons rice-wine vinegar
2 teaspoons cornstarch
6 scallions, trimmed and sliced
1 red bell pepper, seeded and thinly sliced
1 yellow bell pepper, seeded and thinly sliced
salt and pepper
boiled egg noodles, to serve

method

1 Place the turkey in a shallow, nonmetallic bowl and add the ginger, garlic, five-spice seasoning, and half the oil. Stir well, then cover and marinate in the refrigerator for 1 hour.

2 Mix the coffee, teriyaki sauce, honey, vinegar, and cornstarch in a small bowl. Cover and set aside.

3 Heat the remaining oil in a large wok until almost smoking. Remove the turkey from the marinade, add to the wok, and stir-fry over high heat for 3–4 minutes, until brown. Add the scallions, red bell pepper, and yellow bell pepper and stir-fry for an additional 1–2 minutes.

4 Pour in the coffee mixture and continue stir-frying for 1–2 minutes, until the sauce has thickened and coated the turkey and vegetables. Season with salt and pepper and serve with noodles.

chili espresso rub

ingredients

makes about ⅓ cup

2 tablespoons packed dark
  brown sugar
1 tablespoon ground
  espresso coffee
1 tablespoon ground coriander
2 teaspoons ground cumin
1 teaspoons ground ginger
1–2 teaspoons crushed red pepper
  or chili powder
salt and pepper

method

1 Mix all the ingredients in a small bowl until thoroughly combined.

2 Rub the mixture thoroughly into meat, poultry, fish, or seafood up to 6 hours before cooking.

3 Put in a shallow dish, cover tightly, and chill in the refrigerator until required.

chili with coffee

ingredients

serves 4

1 tablespoon olive oil
1 red onion, chopped
2 garlic cloves, chopped
1 pound ground round beef
1½ tablespoons hot chili powder
½ teaspoon ground cumin
1 teaspoon dried oregano
1 cup strong black coffee, cooled
1 (14½-ounce) can diced tomatoes
2 tablespoons tomato paste
1 teaspoon sugar
1 cup canned red kidney beans,
    drained and rinsed
salt and pepper

to serve

sour cream
chopped fresh green chile
tortilla chips

method

1 Heat the oil in a large, deep skillet, add the onion and garlic, and sauté for 5 minutes. Add the beef and cook over high heat for 8–10 minutes, stirring frequently, until browned all over.

2 Stir in the chili powder, cumin, and oregano and cook for 1 minute, then add the coffee, diced tomatoes, tomato paste, and sugar. Season with salt and pepper and stir. Add the beans and cook, uncovered, for an additional 10–15 minutes.

3 Spoon into warm bowls, top with spoonfuls of sour cream and some chopped chile, and serve immediately with tortilla chips.

coffee & walnut bread

ingredients

makes 1 loaf

vegetable oil, for greasing
1½ cups whole-wheat bread flour,
    plus extra for dusting
1⅔ cups white bread flour
1 teaspoon salt
1 teaspoon active dry yeast
¾ cup coarsely chopped walnuts
1¼ cups lukewarm water
1 tablespoon instant
    coffee granules
1 tablespoon olive oil
1 tablespoon honey

method

1 Grease a baking sheet. Put the whole-wheat flour, white flour, salt, yeast, and walnuts into a large bowl and mix. Put the water, coffee, olive oil, and honey into a separate bowl and mix. Make a well in the center of the flour mixture and pour in the liquid. Mix with a knife to make a soft, sticky dough.

2 Turn out the dough onto a floured surface and knead for 5–7 minutes, until smooth and elastic. Put the dough into a bowl, cover with oiled plastic wrap, and allow to rest in a warm place for about 1 hour, or until doubled in size.

3 Turn out the dough onto a floured surface and lightly knead for 1 minute. Shape into an 8-inch-long oval and place on the prepared baking sheet. Dust the top of the loaf with whole-wheat flour and slash a curve along the top of the loaf (just off center). Allow to rest in a warm place for 40–50 minutes, or until doubled in size. Meanwhile, preheat the oven to 400°F.

4 Bake in the preheated oven for 18–20 minutes, or until golden brown and the bottom sounds hollow when tapped with your knuckles. Transfer the bread to a wire rack to cool.

drinks

s'mores coffee & chocolate cup

ingredients

serves 4

2½ cups milk
½ cup strong black coffee
8 ounces milk chocolate or
    semisweet chocolate
    (or a mixture), finely chopped
24 pink and white marshmallows
1 tablespoon store-bought
    chocolate sauce, warmed
2 teaspoons finely grated
    semisweet chocolate

method

1 Put the milk and coffee into a saucepan and heat over medium heat until almost boiling. Remove from the heat and stir in the chopped chocolate. Beat briskly until the chocolate has melted.

2 Return to the heat and simmer gently for 1–2 minutes. Preheat the broiler to high. Divide the hot chocolate among four coffee cups or mugs and top with the marshmallows. Place the cups under the preheated broiler for about 1 minute, until the marshmallows begin to brown and melt.

3 Drizzle the chocolate sauce over the tops and sprinkle with the grated chocolate. Serve immediately.

cinnamon mocha

ingredients

serves 6

8 ounces milk chocolate,
   broken into pieces
¾ cup light cream
4 cups freshly brewed coffee
1 teaspoon ground cinnamon,
   plus extra to decorate

to serve
whipped cream
marbled chocolate curls

method

1 Put the chocolate in a large, heatproof bowl set over a saucepan of gently simmering water. Add the light cream and stir until the chocolate has melted and the mixture is smooth.

2 Pour in the coffee, add the cinnamon, and beat until foamy. If serving hot, pour into six heatproof glasses or mugs, top with whipped cream, a sprinkling of cinnamon, and the chocolate curls, and serve immediately. If serving cold, remove the bowl from the heat and allow to cool, then chill in the refrigerator until required. Pour into six glasses or mugs, top with whipped cream, a sprinkling of cinnamon, and the chocolate curls, and serve.

mocha whip

ingredients

serves 2

1 cup milk
¼ cup light cream
1 tablespoon packed brown sugar
2 tablespoons unsweetened
  cocoa powder
1 tablespoon coffee syrup or
  instant coffee powder
6 ice cubes

to serve
whipped cream
grated chocolate

method

1 Put the milk, light cream, and sugar into a food processor or blender and process gently until combined.

2 Add the cocoa powder and coffee syrup or powder and process well, then add the ice cubes and process until smooth.

3 Divide the mixture between two glasses. Top with whipped cream, sprinkle with the grated chocolate, and serve.

hot caramel latte

ingredients

serves 2

¼ cup granulated sugar
⅓ cup water
1¼ cups milk
½ cup hot espresso coffee

method

1 To make the caramel, put the sugar and 2 tablespoons of the water into a small, heavy saucepan. Heat gently until the sugar dissolves, then boil rapidly for 4–5 minutes, without stirring, until the mixture turns to a golden caramel.

2 Remove from the heat and carefully pour in the remaining water. Stir until the caramel dissolves, then return the pan to the heat and simmer for an additional 3–4 minutes, until syrupy.

3 Put the milk into a separate saucepan and heat over medium heat until almost boiling. Remove from the heat, pour in the coffee and almost all the caramel sauce, and whisk until frothy. Divide between two tall latte glasses.

4 Drizzle the remaining caramel sauce over the top and serve immediately.

variation

For a festive winter latte, substitute 2 tablespoons of gingerbread-flavored syrup (available in some supermarkets and online) for the caramel. Omit steps 1, 2, and 4.

coconut coffee cocktail

ingredients

serves 1

1 tablespoon coconut liqueur
1 tablespoon coffee liqueur
1 tablespoon brandy
1 cup freshly brewed hot coffee
whipped cream, to serve

method

1 Mix the liqueurs and brandy in a heatproof glass or mug.

2 Pour in the fresh coffee and top with a spoonful of whipped cream.

amaretto coffee

ingredients

serves 1

2 tablespoons amaretto
sugar, to taste
1 cup freshly made strong
    black coffee
1–2 tablespoons heavy cream

method

1 Put the amaretto into a warm heatproof glass and add sugar to taste.

2 Pour in the coffee and stir.

3 When the sugar has completely dissolved, slowly pour in the cream over the back of a spoon so that it floats on top.

4 Don't stir—drink the coffee through the cream.

hungarian coffee

ingredients

serves 1

2 tablespoons brandy
sugar, to taste
1 cup freshly made strong
    black coffee
1 tablespoon grated chocolate
whipped cream, to serve
cinnamon stick, to serve

method

1 Put the brandy into a warm heatproof glass and add sugar to taste.

2 Pour in the coffee and grated chocolate and stir.

3 When the sugar has completely dissolved and the chocolate has melted, top with the whipped cream and decorate with the cinnamon stick.

4 Don't stir—drink the coffee through the cream.

irish coffee

ingredients

serves 1

2 tablespoons Irish whiskey
sugar, to taste
1 cup freshly made strong
    black coffee
2–4 tablespoons heavy cream

method

1 Put the whiskey into a warm heatproof glass and add sugar to taste.

2 Pour in the coffee and stir.

3 When the sugar has completely dissolved, slowly pour in the cream over the back of a spoon so that it floats on top.

4 Don't stir—drink the coffee through the cream.

coffee hazelnut soda

ingredients

serves 2

3 tablespoons instant
coffee granules
1 cup boiling water
½ cup sparkling water
1 tablespoon hazelnut syrup
2 tablespoons brown sugar
6 ice cubes
slices of lime, to serve

method

1 Make the instant coffee with the water, cool to room temperature, cover with plastic wrap, and chill in the refrigerator for 45 minutes.

2 Pour the mixture into a food processor or blender, add the sparkling water, hazelnut syrup, and sugar, and process well. Add the ice cubes and process until smooth.

3 Divide the mixture between two glasses, decorate the rims with slices of fresh lime, and serve.

rum espresso with whipped cream

ingredients

serves 4

²/₃ cup heavy cream

1¼ cups hot espresso coffee

1 tablespoon rum

2 teaspoons raw sugar,
   plus extra for sprinkling

method

1 Pour the heavy cream into a bowl and whip until it holds soft peaks.

2 Mix the coffee, rum, and sugar in a liquid measuring cup and pour into four small heatproof glasses or coffee cups.

3 Gently drop spoonfuls of the cream into the coffee. Sprinkle with a little extra sugar and serve immediately.

coffee & cinnamon eggnog

ingredients

serves 4

2 cups milk
²/₃ cup strong black coffee
1 cinnamon stick
2 extra-large eggs
¹/₃ cup granulated sugar
¹/₂ cup heavy cream
2 teaspoons ground cinnamon

method

1 Put the milk, coffee, and cinnamon stick into a saucepan and heat over medium heat until almost boiling. Cool for 5 minutes, then remove and discard the cinnamon stick.

2 Put the eggs and sugar into a bowl and beat until pale and thick. Gradually beat in the milk and coffee mixture. Return to the pan and heat gently, stirring all the time, until just thickened. Cool for 30 minutes.

3 Put the cream into a bowl and whip until it holds soft peaks. Gently fold the cream into the egg mixture. Divide among four glasses, sprinkle with ground cinnamon, and serve immediately, or chill for 1–2 hours in the refrigerator before serving.

midnight cowboy

ingredients

serves 1

2 tablespoons brandy
1 tablespoon coffee liqueur
1 tablespoon heavy cream, chilled
3 ice cubes, crushed
cola

method

1 Slowly mix the brandy, coffee liqueur, cream, and crushed ice in a blender until frothy.

2 Pour into a chilled glass. Top up with cola.

fuzzy martini

ingredients

serves 1

4 tablespoons vanilla vodka
1 tablespoon coffee vodka
1 teaspoon peach schnapps
3 ice cubes, crushed
peach slice, to decorate

method

1 Shake the vanilla vodka, coffee vodka, and peach schnapps over crushed ice until well chilled.

2 Strain into a chilled cocktail glass and decorate with the peach slice.

black russian

ingredients

serves 1

cracked ice cubes
4 tablespoons vodka
2 tablespoons coffee liqueur

method

1 Fill a lowball glass halfway with cracked ice.

2 Pour the vodka and coffee liqueur over the ice and stir to mix.

iced coffee with cream

ingredients

serves 2

1¾ cups boiling water
2 tablespoons instant
   coffee powder
2 tablespoons packed brown sugar
6 ice cubes, crushed

to decorate
light cream
whole coffee beans

method

1 Use the water and coffee powder to brew some hot coffee, then allow it to cool to room temperature. Cover with plastic wrap and chill in the refrigerator for at least 45 minutes.

2 When the coffee has chilled, pour it into a food processor or blender. Add the sugar and process until well mixed. Add the crushed ice and process again until smooth.

3 Divide the mixture between two glasses. Float light cream on the top, decorate with the whole coffee beans, and serve.

sweet milk coffee

ingredients

serves 6

6 tablespoons canned sweetened condensed milk, or to taste

6 hot double espressos or strong-brewed Thai coffees

ice cubes, to serve (optional)

method

1 Put a tablespoon of condensed milk (or more to taste) in each of six cups. Pour a hot double shot of espresso into each cup and stir.

2 For iced coffee, fill six tall glasses halfway with ice cubes. Pour a cup of stirred espresso with condensed milk over the ice in each glass.

banana & coffee milkshake

ingredients

serves 2

1¼ cups milk
¼ cup instant coffee powder
2 scoops vanilla ice cream
2 bananas, sliced and frozen

method

1 Pour the milk into a food processor or blender, add the coffee powder, and process gently until mixed. Add half of the ice cream and process gently, then add the remaining ice cream and process until well mixed.

2 When the mixture is thoroughly blended, add the bananas and process until smooth.

3 Divide the mixture between two glasses and serve.

tex-mex coffee

ingredients

serves 1

1 teaspoon packed light brown
    sugar, or to taste
2 tablespoons Kahlúa or Tia Maria
1 tablespoon gold tequila
²/₃ cup hot black coffee
1–2 tablespoons heavy cream
grated semisweet chocolate,
    to decorate

method

1 Put the sugar, Kahlúa, and tequila in a warm heatproof
    glass with a handle. Add the hot coffee
    and stir until the sugar has dissolved.

2 Hold a teaspoon, back uppermost, just touching the
    surface of the coffee. Carefully pour the cream over
    the back of the spoon so that it floats on the surface.

3 Sprinkle with grated chocolate and serve immediately.

espresso galliano

ingredients

serves 1

4 tablespoons Galliano
sugar, to taste
²/₃ cup freshly made strong
   black coffee
splash orange or lemon juice
orange zest strip, to decorate

method

1 Put the Galliano into a warm heatproof glass and add sugar to taste.

2 Pour in the coffee and orange juice and stir until the sugar has completely dissolved.

3 Decorate with the orange zest.

mocha milkshake

ingredients

serves 2

½ cup cold black coffee
1 tablespoon granulated sugar
⅔ cup milk
5 large scoops chocolate ice cream
2 tablespoons store-bought
    chocolate sauce
whipped cream, to serve

method

1 Put the coffee, sugar, and milk into a blender or food processor and process for a few seconds until frothy. Add the ice cream and blend for an additional 30 seconds.

2 Put the chocolate sauce into a paper pastry bag. Snip off the end and pipe half the sauce around the inside of two chilled, tall milkshake glasses.

3 Pour the milkshake into the glasses. Top with swirls of cream and drizzle with the remaining chocolate sauce. Serve immediately.

index